KIDSCIENCE

REAL SCIENCE YOUR CHILD CAN DO

AN ACTIVITY BOOK FOR BC FAMILIES

A project of *ScienceWorks!* by APASE:
Association for the Promotion and Advancement of Science Education
Vancouver, Canada

Canadian Cataloguing in Publication Data

Griffiths, Anthony J.F.
Kidscience: Real science your child can do

Writers: Anthony Griffiths, primary writer, Barbara Moon, Sandra Scott, Allen Wooten; illustrators, Sean Goheen, Anthony Griffiths, Jerrold Connors.

ISBN 0-9699308-2-8

1. Science—Study and teaching—Activity programs. I. Association for the Promotion and Advancement of Science Education. II. Title.

Q164.G75 1999 649'.51 C99-901189-8

If I have ever made any valuable discoveries, it has been owing more to patient attention than to any other talent.

—Isaac Newton

Credits

Project Manager
Winnie Tam

Project Coordinator
Leah Birnbaum

Writers
Anthony Griffiths, primary author
Barbara Moon
Sandra Scott
Allen Wooten

Content Editors
Jolie Mayer-Smith
Norma Evans

Contributors
Bruce Bohm
Richard Cannings
Kirk Hancock
Margaret Holm
Wilf Schofield
John Taylor
Terry Taylor

Copy Editors
Federico Barahona
Alice Birnbaum

Editorial Advisors
Bob Bandoni
Mike Church
Karen Savage

Illustrators
Sean Goheen
Anthony Griffiths
Jerrold Connors

Photographer
Matthew Claydon

Graphic Designer and Typesetter
Joe Clark

Publishing Advisor
Catherine Warren

Publisher
APASE

Acknowledgments

BC E-TEAM

APEG
Professional Engineers and Geoscientists of BC

THE POWER IS YOURS
BC hydro

Viceroy Resource Corporation

SM Blair Family Foundation

Table of Contents

Introduction

Kidscience is an activity book for kids and parents seeking to learn more about their communities through science. It guides families through scientific investigations, experiments and observations to explore questions about the world around them. Linking science to our communities helps develop an awareness of our common environment, its problems and its wonders.

Kidscience is based on the belief that we start questioning the world around us from an early age, and that our initial interest is in our immediate community. Our communities consist of ever-widening circles around us and include our families and friends, our pets, our homes, our gardens, neighbourhoods, towns and province. It is this community that provides an ample supply of fundamental questions that form the context for a sound footing in science.

Why study science? Science is interesting and satisfying in itself but the thought processes used in science are transferable to other walks of life. If we become used to thinking about our world as part of science, we begin to ask questions about religion, philosophy, politics, economics, and ethics. These are skills that are important to any thinking member of society. A scientific approach to life promotes imagination and inventiveness; skills that are in high demand in today's world. Children rarely see how science connects with their own lives; they often see it as a specialized, hard activity done by mysterious others and fail to consider it as a career option. When we look at science as a method of exploring our own communities, practicing science becomes an achievable goal.

Introduction

Science is a life-long learning experience and the activities in this book are designed to be cooperative ventures between parents and children. They combine the disciplines that are most relevant in our exploration of the community: biology, math, astronomy, engineering, geology and geography. Emphasizing the idea that science is all around us, *Kidscience* includes lists of books, websites and places to visit that will provide insight into your investigations. You will find interviews with real scientists in these pages as well; putting a human face on science in BC. With science as your tool, you will set off on explorations and investigations of the world just outside your door.

Audience

Kidscience is designed, primarily, to be a resource for parents who want to extend their children's science exploration. The activities are suitable for kids between seven and twelve years old and should be done with parents' involvement as guide and facilitator.

Layout

About "What's It All About?"

This section introduces you to the general theme of the activity. "What's It All About" describes the science concepts that will be investigated and provides some background information for the activity.

About "What You Will Need"

The materials and equipment you will require for doing the activity are listed in this section. Most of what you'll need will be easily found in your home.

About "Going Ahead"

"Going Ahead" takes you step-by-step through the main activity. There are questions to guide you in your investigation and to encourage observation. Diagrams and pictures illustrate instructions and concepts to help you along the way.

About "Taking It Further"

Additional activities in "Taking It Further" extend the main activity for more in-depth exploration. This section suggests other options for finding out more about the activity's topic.

About "Resource Connections"

The resources that are listed in this section include books that can be found in community libraries or local bookstores and web sites that can be found on the Internet.

About "Curriculum Connections"

This section, at the end of the book, connects you to the learning outcomes of the BC Education curriculum as laid out in the Ministry of Education's Integrated Resource Package (IRP).

The IRP was developed as a guideline for science teaching in BC and is an inventory of the learning objectives for science from kindergarten to grade seven. The science learning outcomes for each grade level that are addressed by the *Kidscience* activities are listed in the chart beginning on page 156. This will help you to link the skills and knowledge gained from the activity to the objectives being met by schools throughout BC.

A Suggestion

You will find that having a small cache of reference books will be handy since you'll use them frequently for the activities. You can spend a fortune on reference books, but don't! Most books can be found at your local library. However, if you want to buy some really useful books, we recommend:

- *Plants of Coastal BC* by J. Pojar and A. MacKinnon. This plant identification book illustrates each plant with a colour photograph. It has sections on flowering plants, trees, mosses and lichens. It contains interesting discussions of the ethnobotany of many plants. This book is part of a series that includes a guide to plants of the BC Interior and of Northern BC.

- One of the following: *Roger Tory Peterson Guide to Western Birds* by R.T. Peterson; *Golden Book of North American Birds*; or *National Geographic Book of North American Birds* published by National Geographic Society. These are all standard bird books with colour paintings.
- *BC: A Natural History* by R. Cannings and S. Cannings. This inspiring book is highly readable and contains useful and interesting information on the plants, animals and geology of BC.
- *Trees, Shrubs and Flowers to Know in BC* by C.P. Lyons and Bill Merilees. A very useful book that makes plant identification easy and fun. It contains excellent line drawings and colour photographs.

1 Observing Birds

What's It All About?

Birds are the most accessible wild animals. They provide you with a great opportunity to watch nature, and to observe and record animal behavior in a scientific manner. In this activity, you will learn about bird behaviour and adaptation.

What You Will Need

- A notebook and pencil
- Milk cartons or jugs to build a bird feeder
- A notebook and pencil
- Wood if you'd like to try some simple carpentry
- Binoculars
- A book on birds (see suggestions below)

Going Ahead

1. Start in the fall when food becomes scarce for birds. If you feed them regularly, birds will make your home part of their daily circuit.
2. Build a bird feeder in your garden or veranda, using a milk carton or jug, scraps of wood, or other simple materials (for some simple design ideas, see 1-1 Bird Feeders).
3. Hang the feeder from a line that is visible from your house. Put it in a place where cats or squirrels cannot get at it. You may need to put up some barriers.
4. Use birdseed to feed the birds. Try to find a good quality birdseed or blocks of suet from pet or speciality bird stores (e.g. Wild Birds Unlimited in Vancouver). Get into the habit of putting food out every day.
5. Observe the activities at the feeder.
6. Record your observations in a notebook. Date each observation. Note the weather at the time of each observation as well.
7. Figure out how many types of birds visit your feeder daily, and also how many of each type there are. Record these numbers every day.
8. Identify the birds you see, using a book on birds from your local library. You can also draw the birds that visit your feeder. Keep in mind that scientists often use drawings to record data, so the artwork does not need to be perfect.
9. Make your observations at different times of

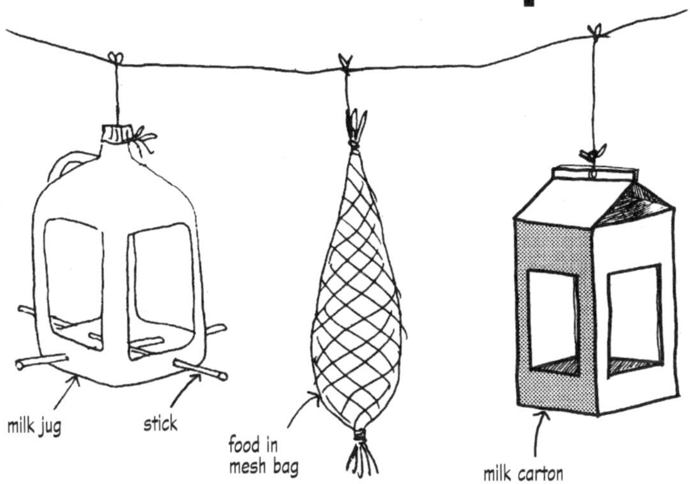

the day, and then review your daily entries. Establish whether there are any differences in the number of birds that visit on different days, or at different times of the day, and whether there are any relationships between the types of birds and the weather. Make educated guesses—or hypotheses—on the possible reasons for any differences observed.

10. Identify specific bird behaviour.
    - Do birds of the same type squabble or fight? What about birds of different types?
    - What are the outcomes of squabbles?
    - Do birds ever hurt each other during squabbles?
    - Is the outcome always the same?
11. If you have friends or relatives in different parts of the province, make this a shared study. Compare notes on the types of birds that visit in different geographic areas.

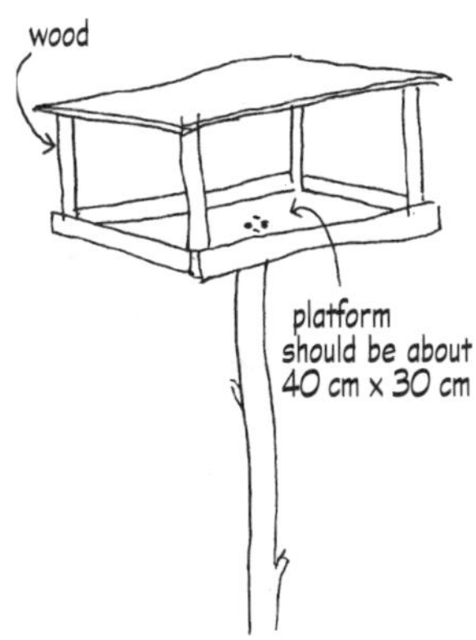

1-1 Bird Feeders

Taking It Further

1. Feed the birds different types of food (i.e. fruit, millet, sunflower seeds, safflower seeds, suet,

cracked corn, peanuts (shelled and unshelled). Place the food in piles or dishes and establish whether different birds prefer different kinds of food. Then compare food preferences with the different types of beak and body size.

2. Make several feeders and place them at different heights. Record which feeder is the most popular with each type of bird. Compare this preference with the type of feet the birds have. Is there is any relationship between their feet and height of the feeder they prefer?

3. Record where the birds fly from to reach the feeder—fence, bush, etc.—and draw a map showing these sites in your notebook. Measure the distances and then provide some new perches closer to the feeder—branches, posts, etc.—and see which are preferred.

4. Build different types of feeders—try different sizes, openings, perches, etc.—and observe what works best for each type of bird.

5. Photograph the birds. Compare the photographs to the pictures in your bird book. Look for similarities and differences.

6. Try recording bird calls on an audiocassette. Match the bird calls with the various birds. Try imitating them to call birds (some stores stock inexpensive bird-calling devices). Birds often respond to a continual swishing noise: pshhh, pshhh, pshhh. Experiment with these calls in the yard, when walking in the neighbourhood or in the park. Do the calls make the birds pop out of the bush to take a look at you?

7. Take a birdwatching walk or hike (early morning or late afternoon is usually the best time). Observe water birds on the ocean or on a lake.

8. Join a birdwatching group.

Resource Connections

- There are various national scientific networks that actively solicit bird feeder data from amateurs like Project FeederWatch. Join thousands of bird watchers who have turned their backyard hobby into valuable research for bird conservation. http://www.bsc-eoc.org
- The National Geographic Field Guide to the Birds of North America
- The Roger Tory Peterson Guide to Western Birds by R.T. Peterson
- Stokes Beginner's Guide to Birds: Western Region by Donald and Lillian Stokes

A Pond in a Jar

What's It All About?

Most of us pass by ponds and ditches unaware that they are teeming with life. You can bring these tiny animals and plants indoors, and reveal a world of interdependence.

Think of an aquatic ecosystem as a miniature model of the Earth. It has only one source of energy—the Sun—which provides all the energy that plants need to grow, reproduce, and produce oxygen. All life depends on plant growth and the oxygen that plants produce.

Many communities contain small and rich pond ecosystems, but sadly they are often seen as muddy nuisances and are drained. The reduction in the number of ponds, in fact, is thought to be contributing to the world wide decrease in frogs and salamanders (animals that are known as amphibians).

Going Ahead

What You Will Need

- A notebook and pencil
- A large tin can
- Plastic wrap
- A large clear jar, like a pickle jar, with a tightly-fitting lid; or large plastic pop bottle
- Plastic buckets or bags
- Scoop nets
- A magnifying lens

1. Look for a pond or ditch the next time you go for a walk. Forests and parks are good places to start.
2. Before you go, build a waterscope:
    - Get a big tin can, and remove both ends;
    - Stretch a piece of plastic wrap or a piece of clear plastic from a bag over one end of the can and secure it tightly with rubber bands (see 2-1 Waterscope).
3. Submerge the plastic end of your waterscope and look into it to observe the pond water. If you look closely, you should see small transparent creatures zooming around.
4. Get close to the surface of the water to see if you can see any organisms swimming around. You might want to dip a plastic bag in the water and look at what you bring up. The water from the

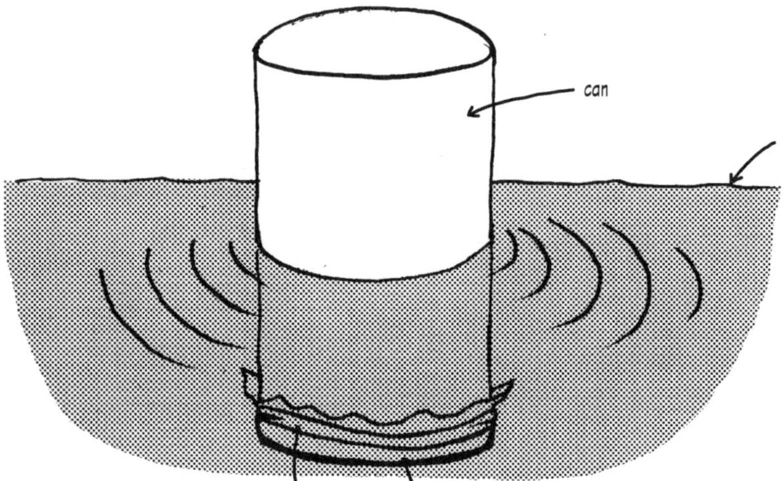

2-1 Waterscope

pond will be full of tiny creatures without backbones called invertebrates, tiny plants called phytoplankton, and bacteria. The bottom mud will be full of interesting larger animals—worms, leeches, snails, flatworms as well as an assortment of insect larvae and eggs. If you use a magnifying lens to look at the plants and animals you will be able to see greater detail. Identify as many organisms as you can, drawing pictures in your notebook.

5. To make your Pond in a Jar, place 2 cm of bottom mud at the bottom of your jar. Collect some pond water in plastic pails or bags. Use the scoop net to catch some of the larger aquatic beetles. Carefully pour the pond water into the jar, making sure you disturb the bottom mud as little as possible. Fill the container about 3/4 full. You can add tap water if you don't have enough pond water. Plant a small quantity of the aquatic plants in the mud bottom (they will grow rapidly). Add a stick

that is long enough to protrude out of the water when it is leaning against the side. This will allow some pond animals to crawl out of the water. Don't be surprised if the water takes several days to clear after you have created your ecosystem (see 2-2 Pond in a Jar).

6. Seal the jar. This will prevent evaporation and ensure that your pond is a closed ecosystem in which the plants and animals are in balance.

7. Place the jar in bright indirect light; an unshaded north-facing window is ideal. Do not expose it directly to sunlight as the heat will kill the animals. You will need to monitor the light conditions carefully to ensure that the ecosystem doesn't overheat and that it is getting enough light. Try not to disturb your ecosystem.

8. Observe the ecosystem every day, or every other day, so you can see the changes in the populations of the small invertebrates. Look at it at night too. Try shining a flashlight into the jar as some animals are more active at night.

9. Use the magnifying lens to examine the organisms in the water, noting their activities. Measure and record how much the plants are growing each week. Think about what is happening in the ecosystem:

- Where are the animals found at different times of the day?
- Where do they go at night?
- Who eats whom?
- How much do the animals eat?
- Do any new organisms appear?

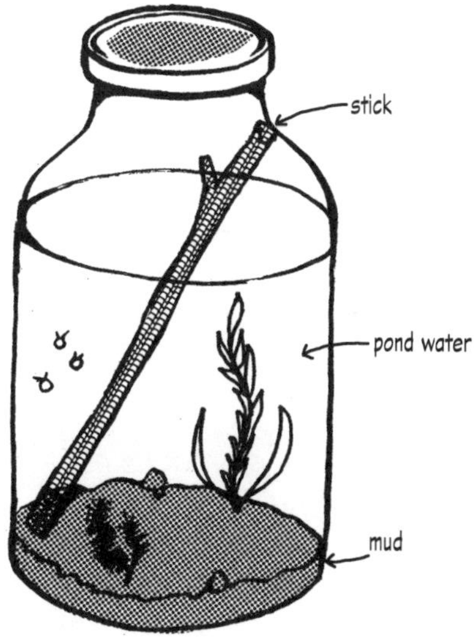

2-2 Pond in a jar

Daphnia (water flea)

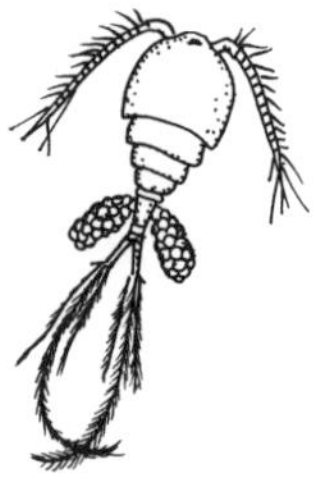

female copepod

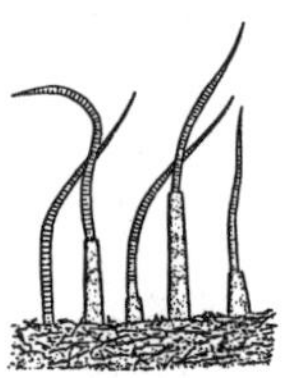

Tubifex

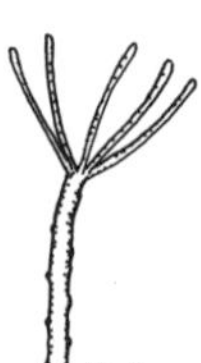

Hydra

Mayfly nymph

2-3 Pond Organisms

- Do the numbers of certain types of organisms appear to be increasing or decreasing?

These are some of the organisms you may see (refer to 2-3 Pond Organisms):

- Water fleas (Daphnia) bobbing up and down as they move. These aren't really fleas and they don't bite. The females can produce eggs on their own without any males. Look for increases and decreases in their numbers.
- Copepods (Cyclops) zooming around or floating. The females will have egg cases that look like baggy shorts.
- Tiny black clam-like dots (seed shrimps) zooming around.
- Leeches swimming or looping along the glass They may only come out at night. (See Activity 24—Fishing for Flat and Bloodsucking Critters).
- White or red worms (Tubifex) with their heads in the mud waving their tails.
- Transparent or green hydra attached to the sides of the jars catching water fleas.
- Snails gliding along the glass. Look for tracks made by the teeth on their tongues as they eat the algae on the glass.
- Eggs laid on the glass or on the plants. Watch them hatch and try to figure out what they are.
- Insect larvae, such as Damselfly and Mayfly nymphs chasing and capturing other species.
- Hollow green balls of Volvox plants rolling through the water.
- Backswimmers looking silvery because they are carrying air with them as they swim upside-down.
- Diving beetles hanging upside-down collecting air at the surface and chasing other animals.

10. Watch for animals that change form. If you see insect larvae turning into adults—or metamorphosing—be sure to release them outside, preferably near a pond.
11. Observe the bottom mud as it develops an orange layer. This is a natural phenomenon that occurs when the bacteria that live in mud reproduce and increase in numbers.

If things go well, your ecosystem may survive for several years. You may wish to add new pond water from time to time to boost the numbers of organisms. If you wish to dispose of your ecosystem, return the components to the original pond or to a local watery ditch.

Things to watch out for:

- Overheating, which will cause everything to die and turn black and stinky.
- Takeover by anaerobic bacteria—they can live in low or no oxygen environments. This is unpredictable and happens occasionally despite all your care and attention. All the components of the ecosystem will gradually turn orange, and sometimes black, as the system becomes anaerobic (without oxygen) and the other organisms die.
- If the walls of the jar become covered in black or brown stains you'll need to scrape them off. These stains are actually colonies of tiny one-celled plants called diatoms that tend to stick together on flat surfaces. Unchecked, they will block the light and the other plants and animals will die, causing the jar to go black.

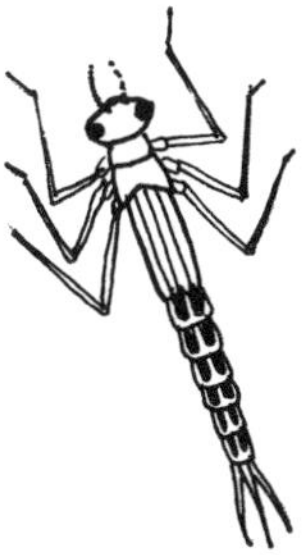

Damsel fly nymph

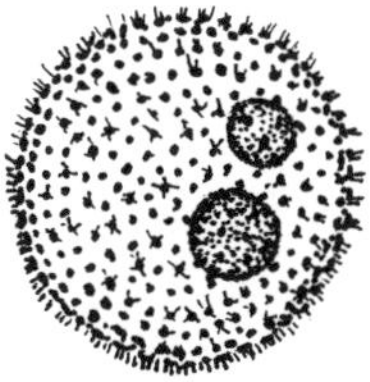

Volvox

back swimmer

diving beetle

2-3 Pond Organisms

Taking It Further

1. Check your local library for books that examine the life cycles of pond organisms.

2. Draw a picture that illustrates the feeding relationships, called the food web, for your ecosystem.

3. Map the distribution of ponds and streams in your neighbourhood or nearby community.
   - Do they all contain the same organisms as the pond you observed?
   - Do the ponds look healthy or polluted?

4. Take a weekend workshop at a local nature reserve that features freshwater habitats.

5. Consider joining a volunteer community group that is working on the health of local streams or ponds (e.g. Stream Keepers).

Resource Connections

- Pond Life by Gerald Cox
- Pond Life: The Young Scientist Investigates by Terry Jennings
- Pond and River by Steve Parker
- Pond Life: A Golden Guide by George K. Reid

Pigeon Plumage

an introduction to genetic diversity

What's It All About?

In this activity, you will observe pigeons more carefully, record their variations, and attempt to deduce their genetic makeup. Pigeons are not native to Canada; they originated from Europe where they were cliff-dwellers which explains why they like to roost in high spots on houses and skyscrapers.

BC pigeons have varied plumage; most of these variations have occurred because of spontaneous changes in the genes. These changes are referred to as mutations, and were considered to be particularly attractive by pigeon fanciers. Some pigeons were bred so there would be more birds with the same plumage variations. At some point, some of these birds escaped into the wild where they began to breed with other pigeons.

Hereditary units (called genes) determine the characteristics of all living things. Genes are parts of chromosomes—long worm-like structures found in our cells—made up of a threadlike substance called DNA (Deoxyribonucleic Acid). Genes are the functional regions along the DNA, and in most big organisms—humans, for instance—every cell in the body contains two complete sets of chromosomes. Hence all genes exist in pairs.

The original pigeon was probably blue— a steely-blue-grey, actually—and had two prominent 'bars' on its wings. Mutations from this original type have resulted in a variety of types that now exist in BC populations. Some of the common mutant types found are checkered wings; red colour—actually a pinkish-beige; grizzled pattern; and solid black (consult 3-1 Pigeon Plumage). However, careful observation will reveal many other rarer types.

What You Will Need

- A notebook and pencil
- Binoculars (useful but not essential)

To keep track of normal and mutant genes, scientists use an alphabetical naming system. Genes are labeled with the letters of the alphabet, and the same letter is used for each of the two genes in the pair.

Let's use the pigeon gene for colour as an example. The normal gene that determines blue colour is represented by the capital letter 'E'. The mutated gene that causes red is represented by the small letter 'e'.

Because the genes are always in pairs, there are three possible gene combinations: 'EE', 'Ee' and 'ee'. In the 'Ee' case, the gene represented by the capital letter (E) 'dominates' the other gene (e) so pigeons of type 'Ee' look blue—exactly like those of type 'EE'. Pigeons that have the 'ee' combination are red in colour.

Going Ahead

1. Note the similarities and differences between pigeons and record these observations. Draw the different types of pigeons in your notebook.
2. Analyze the genetic makeup of two or more pigeons that look different. Begin to describe the genetic features you are observing:

Original	Mutation
c = dark bars on wings	C = dark checker marks on wings
E = bluish colour	e = reddish pink colour
g = not grizzled	G = grizzled (mottled with white spots)
s = not solid black	S = solid black

Note that in one case the original gene is dominant and represented by a capital letter, but in all other cases shown the mutations are dominant.

The complete genetic makeup of any one pigeon type can be deduced as follows (a dash means the gene can be either dominant or recessive):

Type	Relevant genes	Plumage
original type (blue barred)	cc E- gg ss	
blue checkered	C- E- gg ss	
red barred	cc ee gg ss	
red checkered	C- ee gg ss	
grizzled	cc E- G- ss	
solid black	cc E- gg S-	

3-1 Pigeon Plumage

3. Visit a park over a number of days and count the numbers of each type of pigeon in a flock. Each day, list the different types, going from most to least common. Explore whether the percentages are always the same. Repeat this activity in another park or region. Are the same types of birds present and are the proportions always the same?

Taking It Further

Connect pigeon variation with courting practices. Often male pigeons puff their neck feathers and strut around in front of the female as part of their courtship behaviour. Observe one male bird that is doing this. Is he making his advances to only one female? Investigate whether males tend to make advances towards females of similar genetic type (e.g. blue with blue), or opposite genetic type (blue with red). Are pairings more or less random?

Resource Connections

- Discovering Genetics by The American Museum of Natural History England
- Grandfather's Nose: Why We Look Alike or Different by Dorothy Hinshaw Patent
- The Pigeon by Joyce Pope
- Pigeons by M. Schlein

What Weeds May Come

What's It All About?.

Gardeners and farmers tend to think of weeds as a nuisance, but they are simply highly successful plants that do very well in areas where the natural vegetation has been disturbed. Most weeds are plants introduced from other countries that succeed in competition with native plant species. Many weeds have had an extremely negative impact on natural ecosystems. The purple loosestrife has invaded wetlands in BC and other parts of Canada, while the Scotch broom dominates many terrestrial habitats and the Eurasian milfoil weed has invaded our freshwater systems.

This activity will get you thinking about what kinds of weeds are present in your community, and what enables them to succeed. You will explore the annual cycle of plants—how they germinate and grow, and how they compete with one another. This activity requires careful observation and recording over a period of time. You can carry it out by observing weeds in your garden, or on any waste plot.

Going Ahead

1. Early in the spring, select a piece of ground for a weed observation garden. Prepare a 1 m x 1 m area and clear it of all visible plant material. It is important that you get all the roots, stumps, bulbs, and dead leaves out. Dig up the earth to a depth of about 15 cm. If you have a garden sieve, pass the soil through it to remove any remaining organic material. When you have finished, pat the soil down gently so that it is flat.

2. Divide the square into smaller squares, using sticks, string, and pieces of wood (see 4-1 Garden Plot). Draw a picture of your garden plot.

What You Will Need

- A notebook and pencil
- A ruler
- A string
- Wooden or plastic stakes
- Possibly a plant identification book
- A garden sieve

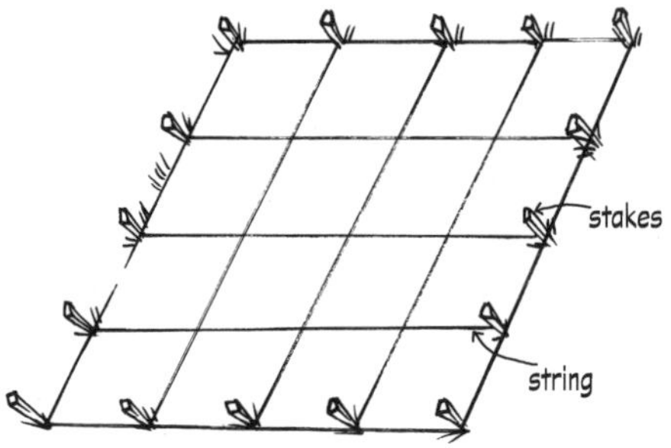

4-1 Garden plot

3. Wait for things to grow, then record the position of the various plants that appear. To facilitate record keeping, assign each plant a number. Draw a sketch of the plants every two weeks, maintaining a record of the changes that appear over time (4-2 Bar Chart shows one way of counting and recording the number of plants).

4. Record the height of each plant you sketch and arrange the results to show which plants grow fastest. One way to do this is to draw a chart of the changes in height over time.

5. Identify the plants as they mature and as new features appear.

- How long did it take before you were able to identify each of the plants?
- What features were particularly helpful in the identification process?

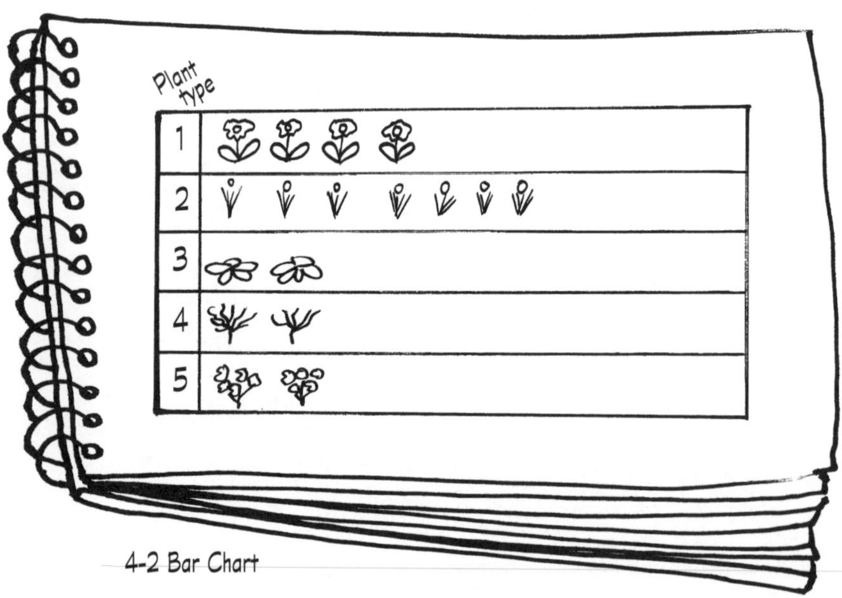

4-2 Bar Chart

6. Using a plant identification book, try to determine which plants are native to Canada and which were introduced from another country.
7. Visit other yards, gardens or parks to observe the types of weeds that are present. Try to determine the types of environments in which certain plants appear to thrive. Identify the features of a plant that might be key to its ability to thrive in a given environment.
   - Do these plants grow only in areas disturbed by human activity or natural disturbances such as landslides?
   - Have you found areas where weeds seem to be competing with native Canadian plants? If so, can you tell which type is winning?
8. When the plants begin to flower and produce seeds, estimate how many seeds each plant will produce.
   - What are the possible relationships between the number of seeds produced and the success with which the weeds are able to grow in a particular environment?
   - Identify other features that might account for the success of some weeds.

Taking It Further

1. Check out the purple loosestrife, a weed that is causing a large ecological problem across Canada, including BC. This plant is not native to BC, but has invaded many areas of the province, radically changing habitats. It is widely considered to be an environmental threat.

There are three types of purple loosetrife plants; the stems and leaves are identical, but the flowers are not. The three types have different lengths of style—the central part of the flower that contains the plant's ovules, or eggs. Each flower type has two stamen lengths—bearing the male pollen (as shown in 4-3 Purple Loosetrife)—which deposit pollen on the backs of bees, and other pollinators, who then carry it to the styles of the two other plant types. This promotes outbreeding, or preferential mating, with another plant.

2. Take a trip to the nearest purple loosestrife population—it usually grows in wet areas such as river banks, estuaries and bogs. (You have to do this in the summer months, when this plant is in flower). The flowers are purple-magenta in colour and are born in tall spikes, usually about a metre tall (don't confuse it with fire weed.)

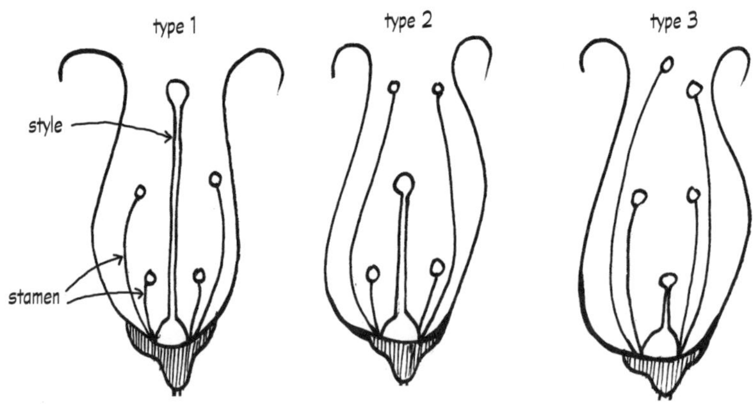

4-3 Purple Loosestrife

3. Examine the plants and learn to identify styles and stamens. Record each plant as having flowers with:

- type 1: long style
- type 2: medium style
- type 3: short style

4. Count the numbers of each type and estimate total proportions.

5. Pick one flower of each type and take it home to draw. Note the colours of the style tips and anthers (stamen tips) in each case. How consistent

are these colours?

6. If possible, pull up one entire plant, including the roots, and take it home to draw. How difficult was it to pull it up? Why (examine the roots)? How easy would it be to eradicate this plant from the area you studied?

7. Note the type of environment in which your plants were growing. Categorize in terms of
   - wetness (normal, damp, soggy, standing in water)
   - terrain (pond, estuary, river bank, stream bank, etc)
   - other plants and animals found in the same environment (which the loosestrife might be outcompeting).

8. Check out the Scotch broom, a bush with bright yellow pea-like flowers, blooming in May. It was first introduced in the Victoria area in the 19th century by someone who was feeling homesick for Scotland. Now the plant has spread widely and is threatening native habitats.

9. Monitor broom populations to find out where it grows. Map the plants in one area, then see how the numbers change over the years. Which native plants are being threatened? After studying the plant for a season, try to deduce the secret of the success of the Scotch broom.

Resource Connections

- Field Guide to Noxious Weeds and Other Selected Weeds of British Columbia by Roy Cranston
- Wildly Successful Plants: A Handbook of North American Weeds by Lawrence J. Crockett
- Common Weeds of Canada: A Field Guide by Gerald A. Mulligan

5 Tree Charting

WHAT'S IT ALL ABOUT?

Trees beautify your neighbourhood and produce the oxygen you breathe. They also provide homes for many animals, plants and fungi. In this activity you will learn to identify different types of trees and recognize which ones are native to BC and which ones were introduced from elsewhere. You will also learn different methods of mapping trees and gain some basic knowledge of tree biology.

What You Will Need

- A notebook and pencil
- A tape measure
- A newspaper
- A knife
- A magnifying lens
- A protractor
- A piece of cardboard
- A tree identification book (available from most libraries)

GOING AHEAD

Sometimes it is difficult to decide whether a plant should be classified as a bush, a shrub, or a tree. Because young trees often look shrubby, this can cause difficulties for biologists. For the purposes of this activity, we will call a plant a tree if it has one main woody trunk with relatively few branches near the bottom and many branches with leaves higher up.

1. Start by looking closely at the trees in a particular area. Your own neighbourhood, a small park, or natural treed area will work well. Try not to choose an area that is too big or daunting. Go for a walk around the neighbourhood to examine the various types of trees.

2. While most trees have certain common features, every type is unique. Think about what appears to make one type—or species—of tree different from another. Examine the colour and texture of the bark, height, amount of branching, angle of branching, leaf shape, leaf arrangement, leaf colour, flowers and fruits. Record a list of all the tree features you notice. A chart like the one below may help to organize the observations:

	bark colour	bark texture	leaf shape	leaf arrangement	leaf colour
1					
2					
3					

You can also look at branch patterns, the shape of the crown of the tree (the mass of leafy branches), the type of flowers produced, and anything else that distinguishes a tree from the rest. Try to identify what you think are the general categories into which we can classify trees.

3. Draw rough sketches illustrating the different types of trees you have seen.

4. Draw a map of the area and record where the various trees are found. If you find lots of one type in a particular area, then show them as a group of trees on the map. If there are lots of different kinds, you might want to consider developing a key, or guide, to indicate where they are located. Test the map with a friend or family member. Can they find the trees indicated on the map?

If you are mapping an open area, like a park, try a surveyor's approach (see 5-1 Mapping Trees in an Open Area). Make a round disc out of cardboard and divide it into 360 degrees (mark positions of 0, 10, 20, 30....360 degrees). Make a cardboard arrow the same diameter as the disc. Use a thumbtack to attach the arrow and the disc onto the end of a stick (at right angles to it) and drive the stick into the ground. For each tree to be mapped, point the arrow towards it and record the position of the tree in degrees. Now walk to the tree and record how far it is in paces. Hence for each tree you have the angle it is seen at and its distance. These measure-

5-1 Mapping Trees in an Open Area

ments can easily be converted onto a map on paper (for an example, see 5-2 Tree Map).

5. Look more closely at a tree that you find particularly interesting. Focus on the general shape of the tree and how the branches are distributed. Note the shape and size of the leaves and fruits. Are the leaves in pairs, opposite each other, or do they alternate up the stem? Record your observations by drawing a leaf in your notebook. If drawing the leaf is too difficult, place a piece of paper over the leaf and rub a soft pencil across the paper to bring out the leaf shape. The same can be done for the bark.

6. Observe how the tree changes over time.
   - Do the leaves change colour, or size?
   - Do the leaves fall off? Do any remain attached?

Some types of trees keep their leaves all year long (evergreens) while others drop their leaves in the fall (deciduous trees). Conifers (cone-bearing trees) are mostly evergreen—Christmas trees, for instance. Most deciduous trees have broad leaves, whereas conifers have narrow needle-like or scale-like leaves.

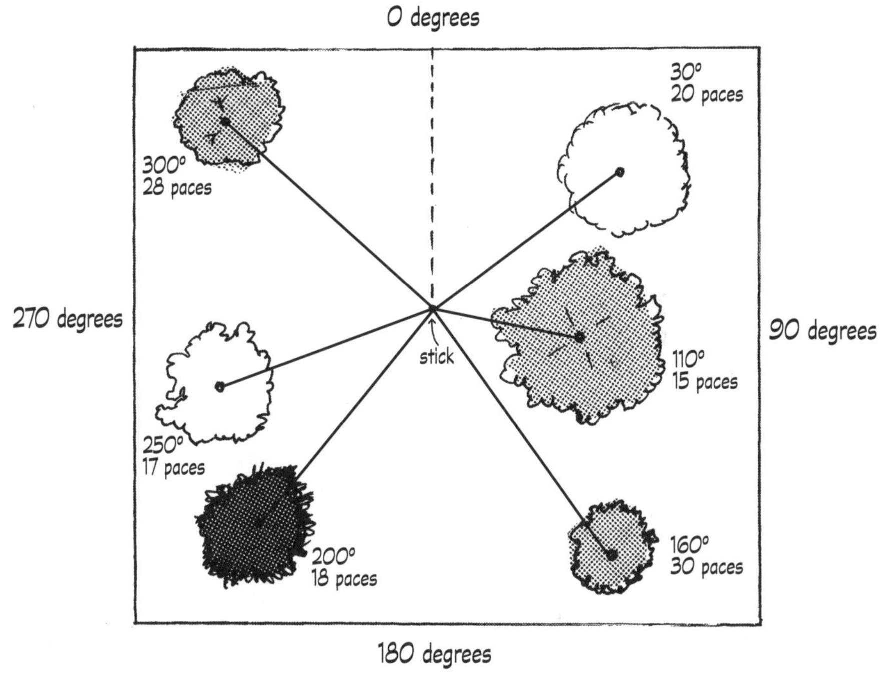

5-2 Tree Map

Taking It Further

1. Find a tree identification book with lots of pictures. Try to decide if any of the illustrations resemble the trees in your community. You don't have to learn the botanical names for all the trees.
2. Compare the trees you see with the trees in a different area. What are some reasons for the differences between the trees in different locations?
3. Find out what trees grew on your block before buildings were built. Think about how you might be able to figure this out (try examining nearby natural areas for clues).

4. Trees have their very own animal communities. Look for the organisms that live on them. Go beyond birds and squirrels and scrape the surface of the bark. Collect the scrapings on a piece of newspaper, examining them closely for tiny plants and animals. You may find a magnifying glass useful. Record your findings and speculate as to how these organisms get their nutrition. Look carefully at the undersides of leaves and branches to find insects. Try 'beating' the branches over a sheet of newspaper to see what insects fall out (this is a time-honoured method used by all professionals and amateurs who study insects). Draw some of the insects in your notebook.

5. Trees grow from seeds.
   - What do the seeds of a particular type of tree look like?
   - Where are seeds found on the tree?
   - Are the seeds present year-round or only at certain times?
   - How are they dispersed? By animals? By the wind?

6. Calculate the height of a tree. Here's how: place a stick in the ground and measure its height and the length of its shadow. Now measure the length of the shadow of a tree. The height of the tree can be calculated as follows (see 5-3 Measuring the Height of a Tree Using Shadows):

- Height of tree = (Height of stick) multiplied by (length of the tree shadow), all divided by (the length of the stick's shadow).

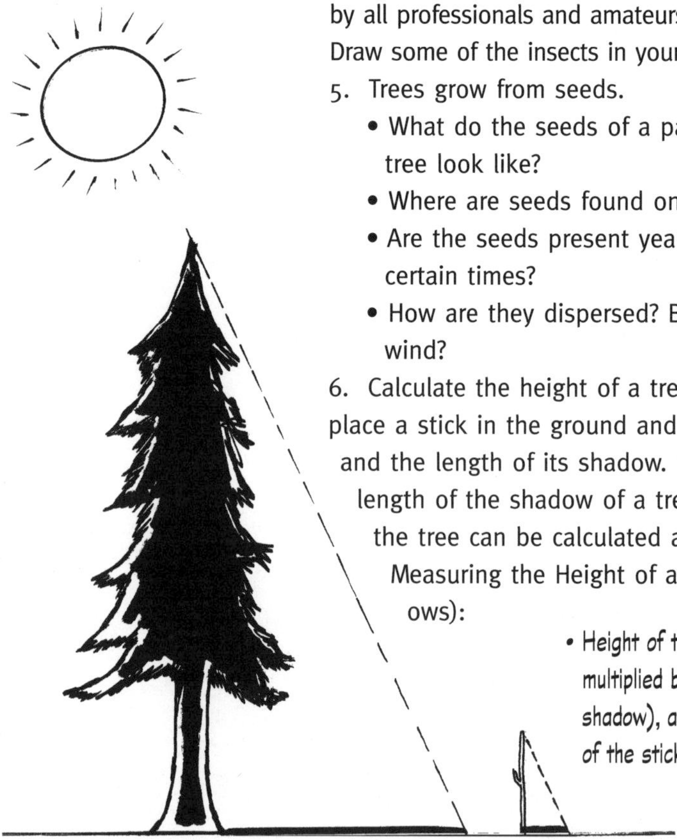

5-3 Measuring the Height of a Tree Using Shadows

For example, if your stick is 30 cm long, the tree's shadow is 1000 cm long and the stick's shadow is 20 cm long, then:

Height of Tree = (30 x 1000) / 20

Height of Tree = 30000 / 20

Height of Tree = 1500 cm or 15 m

Mathematically, this is true because in triangles with the same angles (similar triangles), the ratio of any two sides is always the same.

Another easy way to measure a tree is to stand 50 to 100 metres away from it and ask a friend, whose height you know, to stand under the tree. Hold a stick up at arm's length and line your friend up with the stick, making a mark on the stick (see 5-4 Measuring the Height of a Tree With a Friend). Next mark the height of the tree on the stick, then the width, trunk and any other measurement needed. Then simply do the following calculation, which basically asks how many 'friend lengths' the tree is:

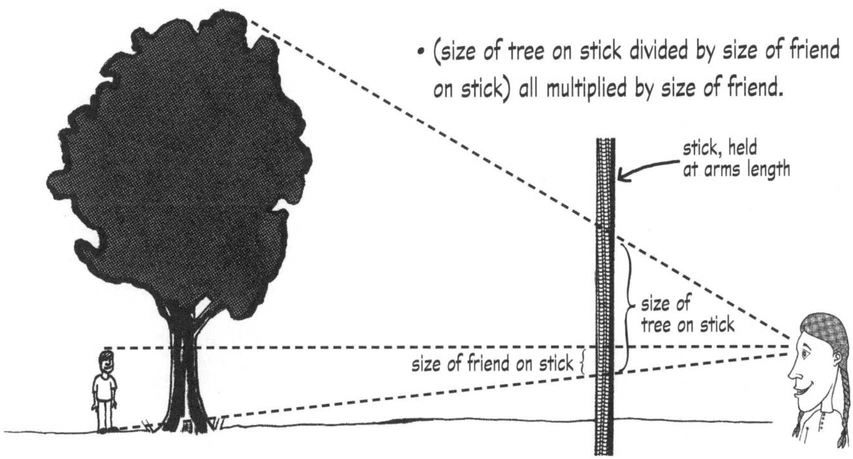

Example:

Height of friend = 2 m

Size of tree on stick = 24 cm

Size of friend on stick = 3 cm

Therefore height of tree = (24 / 3) x 2

= 8 x 2

= 16 m

5-4 Measuring the Height of a Tree With a Friend

7. Spot the 'top ten' trees of BC. The following list combines the trees that are the most common, the most economically important, and the most unique to BC.

This is a hunt that can be done over the long term.

The 'top ten' trees in BC are:

- Douglas Fir. (Coast and interior). Look for 'snake tongue'-like structures sticking out between the scales of the cones. See 5-5 Douglas Fir.
- Western Red Cedar. (Coastal). Flat scale-like leaves; trunk has stringy bark and is flared at the base. See 5-6 Western Red Cedar.
- Western Hemlock. (Coastal). Small cones; tree has droopy tip. See 5-7 Western Hemlock.
- White/Engelmann Spruce (Interior). Typical spruce cones; when a spruce needle is rolled between the fingers the square shape is obvious. See 5-8 White Spruce.
- Ponderosa Pine. (Southern interior). Reddish flaky bark; long needles and big cones. See 5-9 Ponderosa Pine.
- Red Alder. (Coastal). Grey bark with conspicuous 'eyes.' See 5-10 Red Alder.
- Trembling Aspen. (Interior). Heart-shaped leaves that wobble in the wind because of a flat leaf stalk. See 5-11 Trembling Aspen.
- Big Leaf Maple. (Coastal). Big 5-pointed maple leaves. Large flower clusters hanging down (seen in May). See 5-12 Big Leaf Maple.
- Lodgepole Pine. (Coast and interior). Tall, thin crown. See 5-13 Lodgepole Pine.
- Subalpine Fir (all over BC at subalpine elevations). Spire-like shape; cones stick upwards. See 5-14 Subalpine Fir.

Resource Connections

- The Kids Canadian Tree Book by Pamela Hickman
- Shrubs and Flowers to Know in BC by C.P. Lyons
- Tree Book: Learning to Recognize Trees of BC by Roberta Parish

5-5 Douglas Fir

5-6 Western Red Cedar

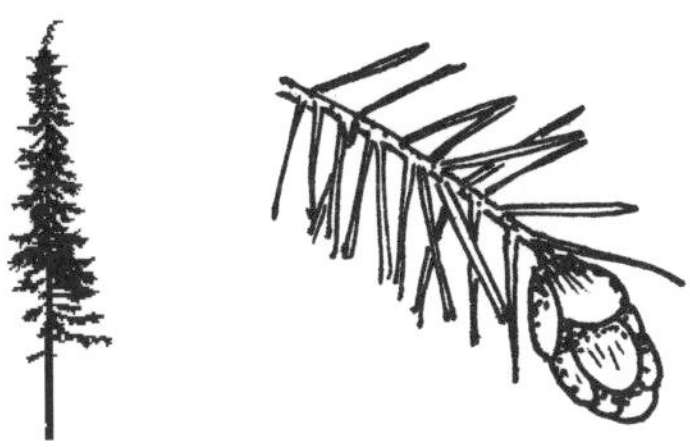

5-7 Western Hemlock

5-8 White Spruce

5-9 Ponderosa Pine

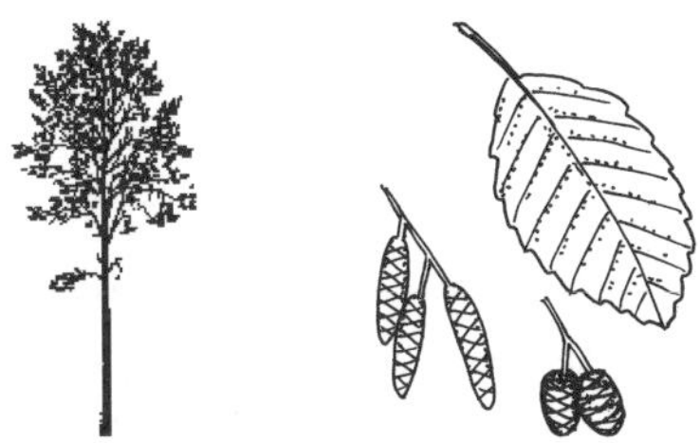

5-10 Red Alder

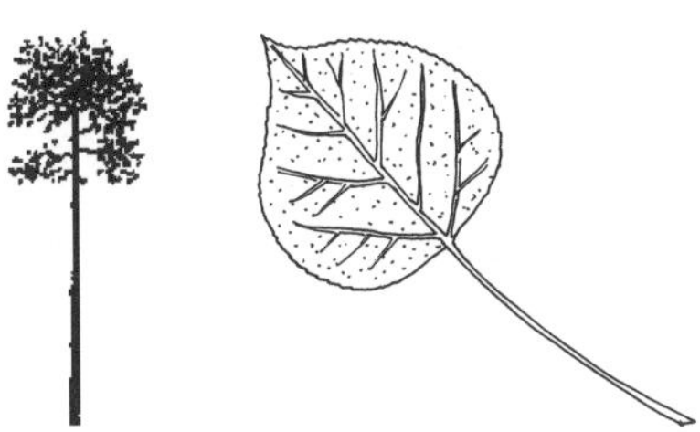

5-11 Trembling Aspen

5-12 Big Leaf Maple

5-13 Lodgepole Pine

5-14 Subalpine Fir

6 The Lay of the Land

What's It All About?

This activity asks you to consider the origin of the mountains, hills and valleys of your community. Geologists call these features 'landforms'. BC is one of the best places in the world to observe a diverse array of landforms—it's a huge outdoor laboratory.

Going Ahead

1. Describe the lay of the land of the block where you live. Is it part of a hill? A valley? Is it flat? Is there water?
2. Take a walk around your neighbourhood. Sketch a map showing hills, valleys, streams, ocean beaches, rocky outcrops, etc. Make a note of any unusual features that you encounter.
3. Using plasticene, playdough, or papier maché, try to make a relief model of your area.
4. Here are some explanations for some landforms you may find:
    - Steep valleys and gorges are chunks of land cut by the eroding effects of active streams of water. Is there a river present now? Could there have been one at some time? Does the river flood? What is the source of the water in the river? Can you find evidence of water erosion (undercut banks or smooth rocks)?
    - Hills are mountains—or volcanic cores—that have weathered away. They may also be rubble left behind by ancient glaciers.
    - Cliffs are sometimes the result of rock upheaval at a fracture in the Earth's crust. They can also be the result of water action of an ancient ocean, or the result of glacial erosion (this is the case with the Stawamus Chief near Squamish).
    - Lakes and ponds are water in a natural

What You Will Need

- A notebook and pencil
- A map
- A magnifying lens
- A book about local geology
- Plasticene or papier maché

basin. Look for places where water flows in and out. Is the lake natural or made by humans? How can you tell?

- Flatlands are sometimes silt from a river delta. (Richmond and Delta are areas formed by silt deposited by the Fraser River.) They can also be the former bed of an ancient river, lake or ocean. Dig under the soil in your garden to look for clues about the origin of the flatness.

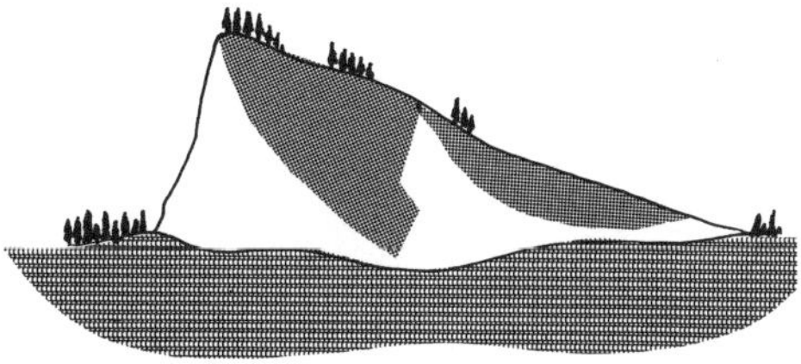

6-1 Fault block

- Smooth-sided valleys were scooped out by ancient glaciers. Much like a river bottom, they acted as huge grinders that left piles of debris (moraines) behind, particularly along its sides (lateral moraines) and ends (terminal moraines). On the coast, look for steep-sided fjords with smooth sides that might have been scooped out by glaciers. Watch for glacial striations—huge glacial skid marks—on exposed rock surfaces which will tell you the direction of the ice sheet's movement.
- Hanging valleys are areas that were also scooped out of mountainsides by glaciers.
- Kettle lakes are land depressions, occupied by water, that were created when glacial ice-blocks melted and left sediment around it.

6-2 Horn

These are the main mountain types: (see 6-1—6-4):

- Fault block mountains formed as raised blocks of the Earth's crust.
- Horns formed after glaciers flaked away mountain tops, leaving a sharp crag.

- Volcanic cores are the centres of extinct volcanoes.
- Folded ridgeback mountains formed by the Earth's crust folding in ripples like a rumpled tablecloth.

Some specific regional observations:

- The Fraser Valley—a floodplain—built up after the last ice age ended 10,000 years ago. It starts near Chilliwack and goes all the way to Tsawwassen. The dome-shaped hills in the valley, like Sumas Mountain, were once islands and retain some of the plants of the Gulf Islands. You can get a good view of the Fraser Valley from the roads to the Cypress, Grouse, and Seymour ski areas, and also from Sumas mountain.

6-3 Volcanic core

- Gravel deposits in the Fraser and Thompson river canyons are located between Hell's Gate and Spences Bridge.
- Multicoloured volcanic rocks—red, green, orange—form the bluffs of the Ashcroft area and of the Cariboo Highway, north of Cache Creek.
- Huge granite intrusions—pushed-up domes—form the slabby and steep peaks that are visible above the Great Bear snowshed of the Coquihalla highway up to the tollbooth plaza.

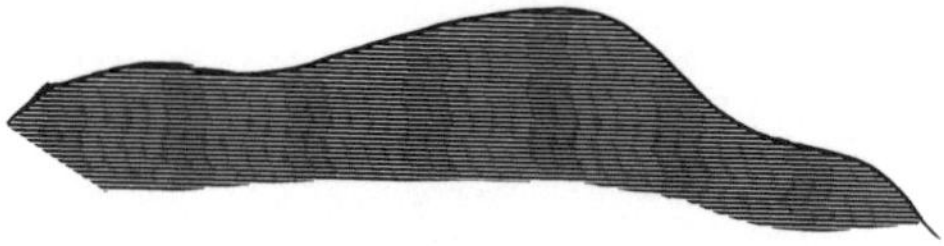

6-4 Folded ridgeback

- Ancient glacial lake terraces form many of the flat benches that flank Okanagan Lake. These are ancient lakefloor deposits in a valley whose centre was once occupied by glacial ice. Lake Okanagan is a huge kettle.

- Large roadside outcrops of crushed, folded, and metamorphosed (changed) rock line the roadway from Salmon Arm to Revelstoke.
- The fold and thrust of the Rocky Mountains, where the crust of North America has been peeled and stacked by tectonic forces, can be seen from any of the highways that cross from BC into Alberta.
- Huge dormant volcanoes dot the landscape, including Mount Garibaldi (near Whistler), Black Tusk (near Whistler), Mount Edziza (central BC), Mount Baker (Washington State).
- Hydrothermal vents, better known as hot springs, also dot the province. These include Harrison Hot Springs and Radium Hot Springs.
- The largest copper mine in BC is HVC Copper, located near Logan Lake in the Kamloops area. This mine is so large, it's visible from space. The company runs tours and there is a viewpoint.
- Historic Barkerville is a great park where a gold mining town flourished during the gold rush of the late 1800s.
- Located in Vancouver, Siwash Rock is a small volcanic core (solidified lava made prominent by the erosion of terrain around it). On the cliffs near Siwash Rock, underneath Lions Gate Bridge, there's a volcanic outcrop that contains hexagonal columns of columnar basalt. Queen Elizabeth Park is a larger volcanic core whose rock was quarried, leaving the bowl that today is the sunken garden. The small hill just to the west of Lions Gate Bridge, on the West Vancouver side, is an old volcanic core that is now covered with houses. Siwash Rock is a side vent of this same

volcano.

- The Department of Highways has erected roadside historical markers throughout the Province; many of these relate to mining and geology.
- The Point Grey peninsula in Vancouver has a solid rock core, but it's covered by several deep layers. The first layer is composed of fine silt and sand from river sediments created before the last ice age. The second layer is made up of rougher material deposited by the last glacier that covered Vancouver. A good place to observe these layers is Wreck Beach or Tower Beach, below the University of British Columbia.
- The Barrier, located on the trail to Black Tusk Meadows, is a wall of lava hundreds of feet high, created by an erupting Mount Garibaldi and stopped by a glacier in the valley below.

Resource Connections

- *Geology of BC: A Journey Through Time* by Sydney G. Cannings
- *Landforms of BC: A Physiographic Outline* by Stuart S. Holland
- *The Geology of Vancouver, The Geology of South Vancouver Island, West Coast Fossils* are available from the Geological Survey of Canada book and map sales: 101-605 Robson Street , Vancouver; telephone (604) 666-0529.

Taking It Further

1. While on family trips and vacations, observe the land.
2. Local natural history groups often run geology hikes. Contact them through your library or community centre.
3. College and university geologists and geographers will generally answer specific questions about landforms.

Meet a Scientist

Kirk Hancock is a geologist.

What do you do?

My areas of expertise are geology, exploration and mining. I use my knowledge of rocks, minerals and earth processes to look for mines. In my work, I oversee and plan exploration programs in various parts of the world. I write reports and compile information to understand the geology of each property. So far I have worked in western Canada, the western United States, as well as Honduras and Mexico. I get to see many different people and where they live. I do a lot of 'on the ground' exploration. This involves traveling by foot, and looking at all the rocks in the properties I am investigating. The terrain can be anything from flat, prairie-like plains, to steep mountains surrounded by glaciers, to thick jungle, to wet rainforests, to dry deserts. I work and live in anything from towns to remote camps. I am often away from home for weeks or months at a time.

What made you want to be a geologist?

I chose my field because I like the outdoors. I enjoy living and working in the countryside which is where I do most of my work. Not only do I learn about the rocks, I learn about the plants and animals that live in the countryside. Geology is like detective work; I look for answers based on a variety of clues. The clues are old so it is a lot like examining ancient history. My work is similar to assembling a jig-saw puzzle with many of the pieces missing. I do my best to put the pieces in their place and fill in the blanks, using information I have gathered, as well as my own experience. The most satisfying part of my work is finally putting all the pieces together and making a logical story out of what I've found.

Tell us a story about an exciting time or event in your career.

Several years ago I worked in the Iskut River / Unuk River area, north of Stewart in northwestern BC. The countryside is mountainous with razorback peaks and broad valley glaciers. I worked there for the whole summer, living in a small camp with five other people. During that time I had the opportunity to walk and climb along the glaciers and walk along the tops of steep mountains. Most of the work required getting picked up and dropped off by helicopter because there were no roads in the region. I often had to use my rock climbing skills to get around as well as my back country living skills. I saw deer, mountain goats, and bears in their natural environment. The most unique experience was watching, from a very safe distance, two wolverine cubs playing on a snow patch in a quiet gully. The little cubs frolicked just like two kittens. It was amazing watching them knowing that, as adults, they could hunt and take down a full grown moose and no other animal in BC would bother them. The opportunities I have to see this kind of thing while I am working are great. Not only have I been able to look for places that might be mined, I have learned first-hand about the wild nature of this province.

How Plants Grow

What's It All About?

Plant growth is key to farming, horticulture, and forestry—all crucial elements of BC's economy. This activity asks you to examine the growth of plants more closely to discover the miraculous life process of plants.

Going Ahead

These steps deal with Amaryllis and broad beans, but you can apply them to any plant.

Amaryllis:

1. Plant the bulb in soil. Keep it moist and place it in a warm place with light. Begin your project once the flower bud has emerged and the stalk is about 5 cm long (see 7-1 Amaryllis).

Bean:

1. Roll up some paper towels and place them inside a jar containing two inches of water. Place the bean in the jar, wedged between the wet paper and the glass (see 7-2 Growing a Bean). Top up the water as it evaporates and never let it dry out. Once the bean has put out its stalk and leaf, allow it to grow about 3 cm and begin the project.

Keep the paper wet and make sure the plant doesn't lean too far into the light. (You may want to monitor the movement of the shoot throughout the day, an interesting study in itself.)

HINT: Whenever you study living things, it is a good idea to study more than one. Plant an extra bulb or bean if you can.

2. Keep track of how your plant grows. To do this, you will need to mark it on various parts—stem, leaves, and even the roots of the beans—with

What You Will Need

- A growing plant! Any bulb, or growing plant, will do. Amaryllis is the most spectacular while broad beans, or any other type of beans, grow quickly
- If you start your own plant, you will need seeds, a pot, some potting soil, and a location near a window, where the plant can get sunlight
- A glass jar
- Paper towels
- India ink and a thin pen nib or brush; or
- A thin permanent magic marker
- A ruler

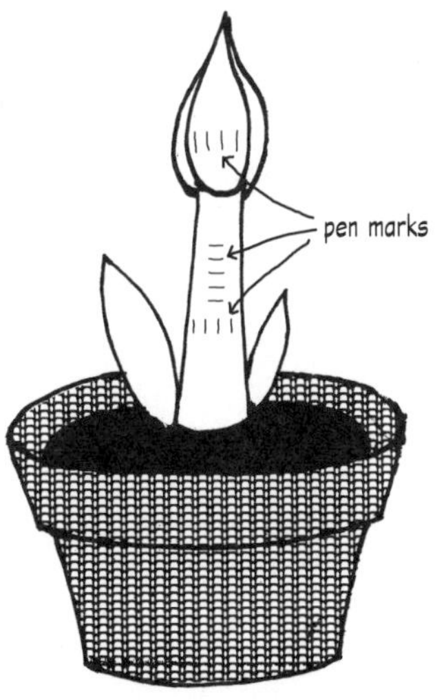

7-1 Amaryllis

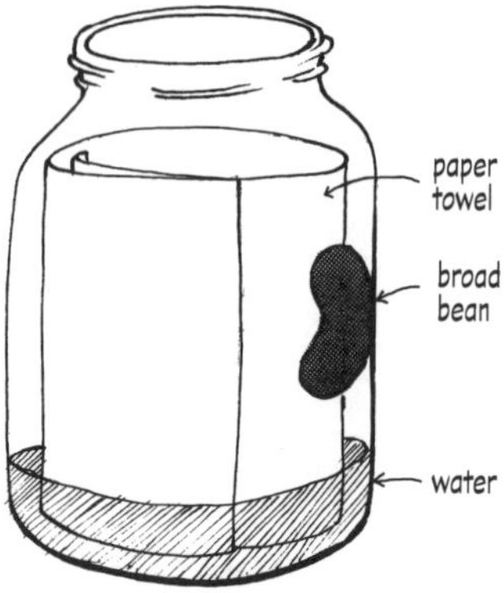

7-2 Growing a Bean

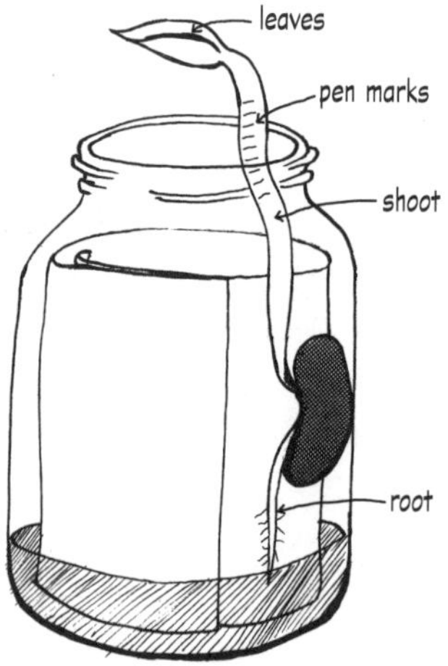

7-3 Bean Sprout

lines spaced evenly apart, say, 5 mm apart (see 7-3 Bean Sprout).

3. As the plant grows, watch what happens to the lines. Record the results with sketches, measuring the distances between the lines.

4. Explain your observations.

- What parts of the plant show no growth?
- Which part shows the fastest growth?
- Is growth occurring along the long axis (length) of the plant, or across the width, or both?
- Calculate the rate of growth in the various marked off regions. How many millimetres does a part grow per week?
- Are your answers to these questions the same for each of your plants, assuming you planted more than one? If not, why not?

Taking It Further

1. Measure the growth of other garden plants; you may have to use paint or nail polish to mark them since rain might wash off the ink. You will obtain the quickest, most interesting results in spring and early summer when plants are growing at the fastest rate.

2. Compare the growth speed of different plants. Which ones grow the fastest? What types of plants are these?

Resource Connections

- Seeds to Plants by Jeffrey Bates
- From Seed to Plant by Gail Gibbons
- How a Plant Grows by Bobbie Kalmann
- Watch It Grow! by Julian Rowe

Getting to Like Lichens

What's It All About?

Because lichens are small and can be easily mistaken for dirt or other stains, we tend to ignore them. Yet they are everywhere. Each lichen is actually two plants combined in one, composed of a fungus, a plant related to mushrooms, and an alga, a simple green plant. Lichens are mostly grey-green in colour; the grey comes from the fungus and the green from the pigment, called chlorophyll, inside the cells of the alga. While the fungus obtains nutrients from the surrounding environment, the alga uses its green pigment to capture the sun's energy. Thus, one partner provides nutrients, and the other energy. In biology, this kind of intimate association is called a 'symbiosis' which means 'living together'.

Lichens are also very sensitive to pollution, so they're good indicators of increasing pollution levels in your community.

Because of their interesting structure and usefulness in assessing air quality, lichens merit a closer look. This activity will allow you to become familiar with different types of lichens, their structure, and the places where they grow.

What You Will Need

- A Notebook and pencil
- Old used envelopes
- A penknife (paint scraper or butter knife will do)
- Possibly a lichen identification book
- Possibly a magnifying lens

Going Ahead

1. Take a look around your garden or block for lichens. Also explore a nearby natural area, like a forest. Lichens are small, gray-green, stemless, crispy-looking structures that grow on trees, walls, and rock surfaces. Lichens can take on a variety of appearances and forms, which help to classify them. There are many different types of lichens, as seen in the table below:

Appearance or form of lichen	Description
Dusts	Dust-like. Often found in dry places under overhangs
Crusts	Paint-like
Scales	Ressembles overlapping fish scales
Leafy	Ressembles small corn or potato chips, often with root-like structures
Clubs	Finger or Golf tee-like; erect structures
Shrubs	Small bush-like; branched structures
Hair	Long highly branched tufts hanging down

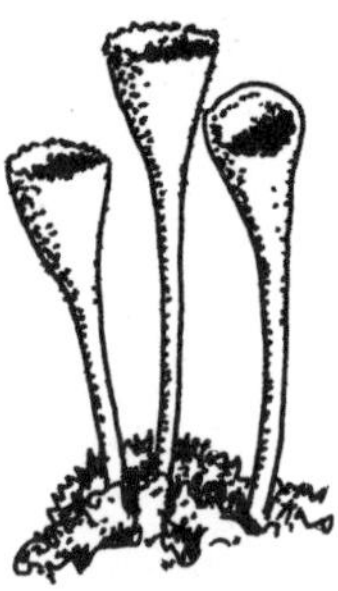

Cladonia

Platismatia glauca

8-1 Specimens of Lichens

2. Collect small pieces of a lichen by scraping it with a knife. Take enough so that you'll be able to recognize the lichen if you see it growing elsewhere. Put the samples into envelopes labeled with the collection place, what it was growing on, and date. Label the samples 1, 2, 3, etc.
Environmental Friendly Collection Tip: Never remove an entire specimen (make sure you leave behind as much as you collect. This will allow the lichen to continue with a healthy life-cycle). Keep this in mind whenever collecting living specimens.
3. Make a list of each type of lichen you find. Sketch your samples and estimate how common each type is, relative to other types.
4. Look for associations between lichens, comparing various samples.
   - Do you see related types?
   - How do they differ?

- In what type of places do they like to grow?
- What is the most unique type?
- What is the biggest type? Smallest?

5. Revisit the different sites where the lichens were found to learn more about where they grow.
6. Become familiar with lichens by trying to learn their names. Using a lichen identification book, try to identify some specimens. Here are some types that are easy to identify. (See 8-1 Specimens of Lichens):
    - Cladonias produce erect structures that look like golf tees and red-tipped lipsticks;
    - *Platismatia glauca*—ragbag—are a common 'rag' lichen found on tree trunks that resemble little torn pieces of grey-green rags with frilly edges;
    - *Parmelia sulcata* produce grey-green flat branching structures with a texture like wax paper;
    - *Xanthorias* are orange cups, cushions, or dusts;
    - *Lobaria pulmonaria*—lungwort—are large, lobed, grey green—or bright green—'leaves' up to 10 cm wide, found only where air is unpolluted;
    - *Lepraria* are dust lichen that are grey green, dust-like, and are often found under dry overhangs;
    - *Usnea longissima*—Methusela's beard—are grey-green, beardlike lichens with long streamers hanging from trees. The central stem has a solid core revealed by pulling back the sheath.

Parmelia sulcata

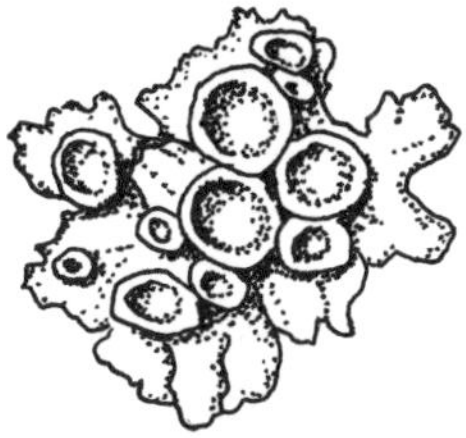

Xanthorias

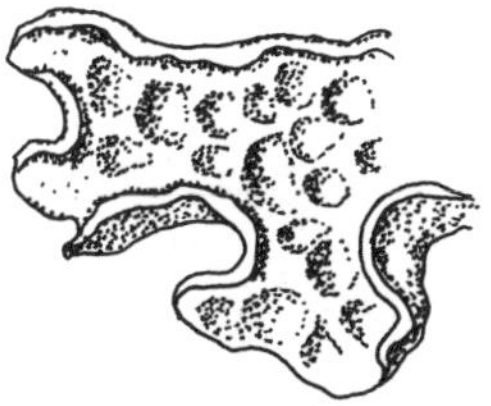

Lobaria pulmonaria

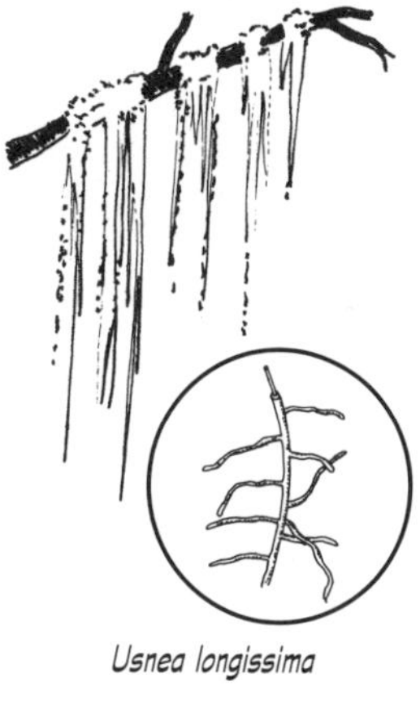

Usnea longissima

8-1 Specimens of Lichens

Taking It Further

1. Lichens can be used to dye wool and cloth. Find a book about this in your local library and try it out. Work with small pieces of wool, so that you don't have to collect a lot of lichen. Lichens grow relatively slowly. If you harvest large quantities, it may take them years to grow back.

2. Categorize lichens according to where they grow.
   - Do certain types of lichens prefer to grow in certain places?

3. Some lichens are very sensitive to pollution; consult your lichen book to find out which types are and aren't. Based on the presence or absence of certain types of lichens, assess the air quality in your neighbourhood.

Resource Connections

- The Lichens of BC by Trevor Goward
- Macrolichens of the Pacific Northwest by B. McCune and L. Geiser
- Plants of Coastal British Columbia by J. Pojar and A. McKinnon
- Mosses Lichens and Ferns of Northwest North America by Dale H. Vitt, J. Marsh and R.B. Bovey

Making a Plant Collection

What's It All About?

Botany, the study of plants, is a fascinating hobby. In this activity you will construct a plant press and use it to prepare a collection of local plants. This is an introduction to plant biodiversity, a key element in environment awareness. This activity allows you to practice recording botanical information and gain skill in plant illustration.

What You Will Need

- Two sheets of plywood, either 1/4 or 3/8 inches thick and 1 foot square
- Up to ten sheets of corrugated cardboard, about the same size as the plywood
- Up to twenty sheets of newspaper, about the same size as the plywood
- Four 4" or 6" stovebolts with wingnuts
- Eight washers
- A drill and drill bit
- A couple of old, large belts (to secure the boards if you don't have bolts and wingnuts)
- White paper
- Sticky tape
- Possibly a plant identification book

Going Ahead

1. Take a walk, bike ride, or drive to the nearest natural area and collect up to 10 healthy plant specimens. Try to get flowers if it is the flowering season, and roots if they are not too big. Remember the specimen has to fit in the press you have made. Wash any dirt from the plants and blot dry. Record the date and the site where the specimens were found. Add a brief description of the plant.

Two cautions:

- It is illegal to pick plants in a park or conservation area.
- Do not pick any plants that appear to be rare.

2. Set up your plant press (see 9-1 Plant Press). Place the plants between two sheets of newspaper and stack them like this:

- wood / cardboard / newspaper / plant / newspaper / cardboard / newspaper / plant / newspaper—and so on (see 9-1 Plant Press).

Don't forget to create a system for recognizing your plants later—jot a number on a bit of paper or on the newsprint, and record this number in your notes. This will make identification much easier when you open your press later on.

Put the bolts on and tighten the wingnuts, so that the plants are firmly pressed between the sheets. Don't over-tighten—this will bend or break

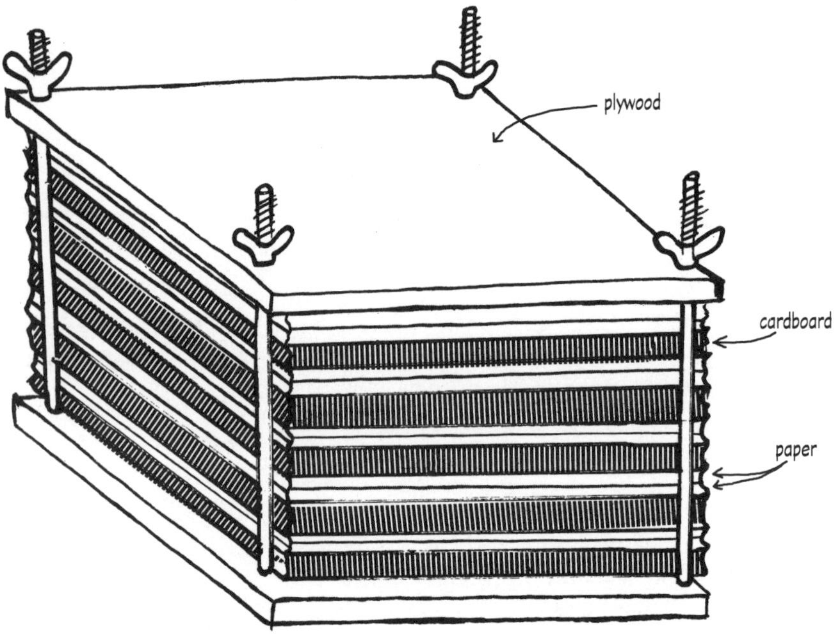

9-1 Plant Press

the boards. If you are using straps or belts, pull them tight around the entire sandwich of boards and plants.

3. Allow the press to dry for a few weeks. Check how the drying and flattening is progressing. Once the plants are dry, remove them and begin the cycle again with new plants if required.

4. Mount the dried, pressed plants on the sheets of white paper, sticking them down with small pieces of sticky tape. Don't forget to write down the number of your plant on the corner of the paper.

5. Identify your plants. This is when your system of recording comes in handy. Refer to your number and notes, and try to identify your plant (if you haven't already done so). Write the plant names on the paper alongside the pressed plant. Write the date and collection site as well.

6. You can store your plants between two large sheets of cardboard, tied up with string. Or you can turn them into a scrapbook.

Taking It Further

1. Take your plant press with you on vacation, and make a collection of holiday plants. Be careful, though. If you go abroad, it is illegal to bring back to Canada any dry plant material if there is dirt on it. Dirt may contain insects or other creatures that may harm local plants. Make sure your plants are completely dry, pressed, and clear of any soil. Compare the holiday plants with the local plants.
2. Join a club to find out more about plants. Local natural history or nature clubs often hold plant hikes.
3. Make greeting cards using dried flowers arranged in pleasing patterns. The plant names could be written on the back of the card.
4. Go to the seashore at low tide and sample the marine plants—seaweeds. Look for small specimens only, as large ones are difficult to dry and store. (HINT: the tiniest ones live on the rocks in tidepools.) The drying process is the same, but you will need to change your newspapers more often to help the plants dry faster—seaweed starts wetter and takes longer to dry.

Resource Connections

- The Kids Canadian Plant Book by Pamela Hickman
- Trees, Shrubs and Flowers to Know in BC and Washington by C.P. Lyons and Bill Merilees

10

Salmonberry Testing

What's It All About?

This activity involves scientific taste experiments with the fruits of the salmonberry plant, *Rubus spectabilis*, which is found everywhere from California to BC and Alaska, as well as in Japan. The berries of the salmonberry plant are either red or orange. A plant will have either all red or all orange berries, but never a combination of the two. The colour variation is genetically-determined and the reason for the coexistence of these colours is not known.

The first activity involves making a fruit dessert using each berry type, then doing an experimental test to determine if there is any detectable difference in taste. This might explain the coexistence of the two types.

This activity must be done in June and July, the months when salmonberry plants bear fruit.

What You Will Need

- A notebook and pencil
- Basic cooking supplies
- Containers for collecting fruit
- Salmonberries

Going Ahead

1. Locate a population of salmonberries. There are only three types of raspberries that grow wild:
   - Thimbleberries are large-leaved and have small, dark, red berries;
   - Creeping raspberries grow on low vines;
   - Salmonberries grow on large bushes up to 2 metres tall and have bright red, or orangey-yellow, blackberry-sized fruits.

   Hence it is virtually impossible to mistake a salmonberry, but even if you do, don't worry—all 3 types are edible.
2. Collect 3 cups each of the red and orange types.
3. Make two fruit cobblers, one for each type of berry.

Recipe (the crust is optional):

In a saucepan, combine:

- 1/2 cup of water

- 1/2 cup of sugar
- 1 tablespoon of cornstarch

Boil for 1 minute. Stir the 3 cups of either red or orange salmon berries and place in a small baking dish. Save a few fresh fruit of each type for further testing.

Make the (optional) crust batter by mixing:

- 1/2 cup of flour;
- 1/2 Tbsp of sugar;
- 1 teaspoon of baking powder;
- 1/4 teaspoon of salt;
- 2 tablespoons of shortening;
- 1/4 to 1/2 cup of milk.

Spoon the crust batter over the top of the fruit and bake at 400 degrees for 30 minutes. Let your cobbler cool and create a labeling system—'A' for bright red, and 'B' for yellow berries, for instance—to help you remember which type of berry went into each cobbler. Record your label system.

4. Blindfold various willing members of the family. Feed them spoonfulls of each coloured cobbler. Write down their comments about each one. Don't let them hear each other's comments as it might influence their opinions. Ask as many people as possible, and combine the results to determine whether the two colours of salmonberries taste different.

5. Repeat the experiment, but this time feed the participants small amounts of raw red and orange berries. Do they notice any difference?

6. Examine your data from this experiment and look for patterns. There are several possible results:

A. Everyone can tell the two forms of berries apart.

B. Some people like one type better than the other.

C. No one can tell the difference.

- What do these results tell you about taste?
- Do you think other animals may have similar preferences?
- What animals eat these fruits?
- What, if any, is the 'survival advantage' of a plant species that has two different colours of fruit?

Taking It Further

1. Establish whether birds can tell the difference between the taste of the two varieties. If they do, what colours do they prefer?
2. Place an equal number of red and orange berries—say 20—into two bowls, and put them in a place where birds come to feed. If you have a bird feeder, use that area.
3. Retire to a safe distance and keep an eye on the dishes. Note whether the birds are feeding from them. If they aren't, you may have to try another location, or time of day. When the birds start feeding, record the types of birds you see.
4. Record how many berries of each colour the birds have eaten. Top up to the original number because you don't want the birds to choose a bowl based on the number of berries in it. Let the birds feed again and record the numbers of berries eaten.
5. Repeat the experiment at the same time on a different day. You can also try different times of day.
6. Decide whether the birds prefer one type of berry over the other. Do you think this type of preference could explain the coexistence of the two colours of fruits?

Resource Connections

- It's the Berries by Marmelade Black
- The Pacific Northwest Berry Book by Bob Kramm
- Wild Berries of the Pacific Northwest by J.E. Underhill

How the Human Body Grows

What's It All About?

Growth is key to any organism's maturation. In this activity, you will study human growth. You will measure family members and correlate measurements with their age and gender. A program of measurement carried over a long time period can show how sizes and proportions change with time.

Going Ahead

What You Will Need

- A notebook and pencil
- A tape measure
- Graph paper

Some body measurements are highly dependent on dietary quality and quantity, so it is best to measure body parts that aren't directly influenced by what you eat. The measurements below are relatively independent of diet.

1. Create a data table in your notebook. For each family member you measure, record the following information:
   - height
   - length of torso (shoulder to groin)
   - circumference of head (just above the ears)
   - length of hand
   - width of hand
   - length of middle finger
   - length of arm (armpit to wrist)
   - length of upper arm
   - length of lower arm
   - length of inner side of leg (standing)
   - length of thigh (knee to groin)
   - length of calf, and length of foot
   - width of foot (at ball of foot)
2. Look for relationships between each measurement and the age and sex of different family members. To do this, first graph each measurement in relation to age (see 11-1 for an example). Do the points in your graph all lie on a single, straight line? If the answer is yes, then growth is a constant value over time. But if the answer is no, then the

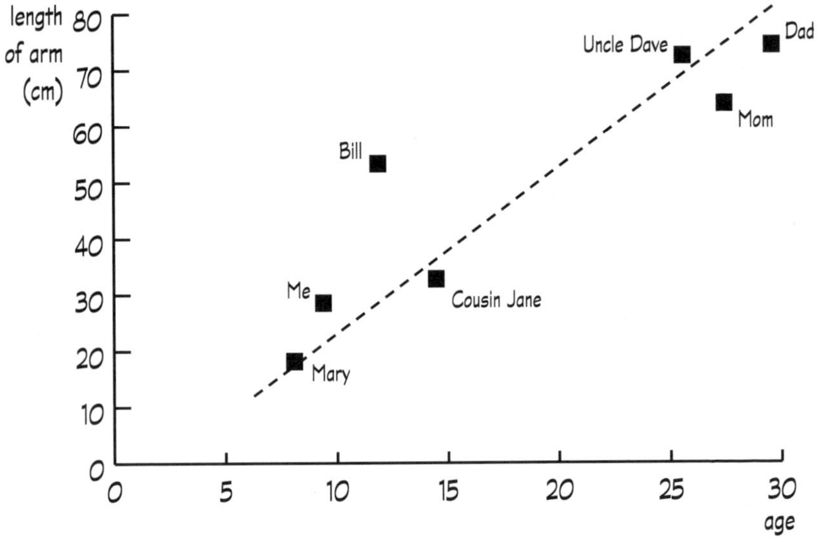

11-1 Example Graph

speed of growth must be different at different ages. Repeat this activity, but this time, graph measurements in relation to sex.

3. Calculate some measurement ratios, and see how they vary with age. For example, hand length might be 20 cm and width 5 cm, so the ratio of the two would be 20 divided by 5 which equals 4. Choose two measurements and calculate the ratio for various family members. Then graph these ratios against age. Do you notice any patterns?

4. Measure siblings and friends at 3 monthly intervals. Graph these against age. When is growth most rapid? Which ratios change the most?

Resource Connections

- From Head to Toe by V.A. Alexandria
- Looking at the Body by David T. Suzuki

Mushroom Spore Prints and Beyond

What's It All About?

Fungi are nature's recyclers. They promote the decay and rot of dead organisms, returning the nutrients to the environment so they can be reused by other organisms. If this didn't occur, dead animals and plants would accumulate. The type of fungus that most of us are familiar with is the mushroom. Mushrooms appear either on the surface of the ground, or as plate-like protrusions—'brackets'—growing on the bark of trees. People are sometimes frightened by fungi, thinking they are dangerous, poisonous, or slimy. Even though a few are poisonous, handling them is not dangerous if you wash your hands afterwards. **Never eat wild mushrooms.**

Mushrooms—and other types of fungus—use spores to reproduce; they don't produce seeds like flowering plants. Spores are reproductive cells that can grow to become a new fungus if they are on the right surface.

In this activity, you will collect spore prints from mushrooms. Experts use spore prints to identify mushroom species.

Going Ahead

What You Will Need

- A notebook and pencil
- White and black construction paper
- A fungus identification book
- Kitchen dishes or plastic tubs
- Hair spray or art spray

1. Find some mushrooms. They generally appear in the spring and fall when the weather is damp. Hike to an empty lot, a forest or wooded area, near your home. Collect about 20 mushrooms in a paper bag.
2. Assign each specimen a number and make a quick sketch showing its size, shape and colour. Record the date and place where you collected each specimen.
3. At home, prepare your spore prints. Cut off the caps (see 12-1 Mushroom Cap). Note that underneath the caps are radial membranes called

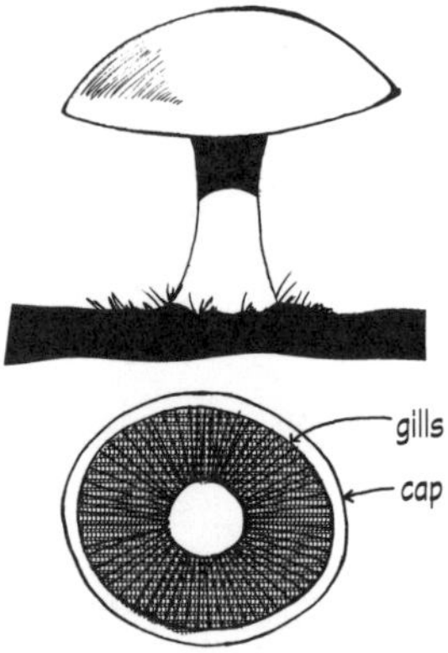

12-1 Mushroom Cap

'gills'—this is where the spores are produced. Pull away any tissue to fully expose the gills, and then place the caps down on the white, or black, paper. Place a dish, cup, or plastic tub upside down over the caps to prevent air currents from disturbing the spore drop (refer to 12-2 Making a Spore Print). Leave the caps on the paper overnight and inspect the paper the next day. If there is no spore print, leave the caps on the paper as long as necessary. If you still don't see any spore print, try using the other colour of paper; the print might show up better. Once you succeed, remove the dish immediately, label the spore prints and give them another day to dry.

4. Preserve your spore prints. Apply hair spray or art spray to attach your spores to the paper. To avoid altering the arrangement of spores, spray from about 30 cm away, letting it fall gently on the prints. Cover them with wax paper if you're not using a spray. Label the spore prints with the specimen number. Glue the spore print into your notebook next to the number and sketch of the mushroom.

Taking It Further

1. Collect prints from mushrooms harvested at different times of the year and from different places. Compare them with your first collection.
2. Identify some of the mushrooms, using a mushroom book that is specific to North America.
3. Look for evidence that will show you more about how mushrooms grow. Remember that mushrooms don't have roots like other plants. Explore the soil around the base of the mushrooms and try to locate the whitish threads that are the underground part of the fungi. These threads absorb nutrients from the soil.

Resource Connections

- Guide to Common Mushrooms of British Columbia by R.J. Bandoni and A.F. Szczawinski
- Mushrooms of Western Canada by Helene M.E. Schalkwyk

4. Record fungal diversity in different places in your neighbourhood. Compare mushrooms found in fields with those found in forests. Do you notice differences in diversity? In the forest, many of the mushrooms live in symbiosis with the roots of trees (these are called mycorrhyzal fungi). They tend to be bigger and more numerous than field mushrooms (these are called saprophytic fungi) which break down dead plant and animal material to obtain nutrients.

5. Compare mushrooms growing near or under broadleaf trees with mushrooms growing under evergreen trees.

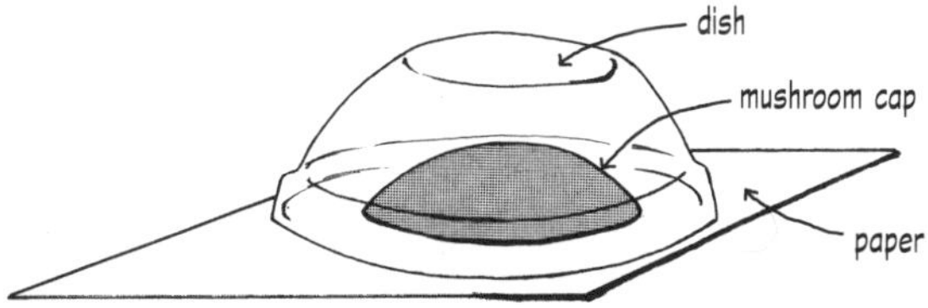

12-2 Making a Spore Print

6. Bracket fungi grow on tree trunks and look like protruding shelves. Compare bracket fungi with other fungi. Some bracket fungi decay the non-living heartwood, while others on the living sapwood are parasitic. Are these bigger or smaller? Do they have stems? Speculate as to why or why not. What are some other differences?

7. Look for small or unusual fungi on the ground. Remove the leaf litter—you might see small 'cup fungi,' small mushrooms, and possibly the whitish threads that fungi are made from.

8. Look for jelly fungi—they look like pieces of yellow or whitish jelly and grow on dead tree stumps, logs or fences—and coral fungi, which grow on the ground.

9. Make an assessment of fungal diversity in the area you studied.

A Sense of Global Position

13

What You Will Need

- A notebook and pencil
- Several pieces of card-board about 15 cm x 15 cm
- Sticky tape
- A protractor
- A ruler
- Possibly a compass

What's It All About?

Ecological awareness is a very important aspect of our appreciation and respect for the world around us. Developing a sense of one's position on the planet Earth is central to the evolution of this awareness. This activity involves calculating the latitude and longitude of your home, so that you can get an idea of your location, relative to the rest of the planet.

Since the Earth is a sphere, we need to use planes and angles in order to accurately measure distances on the Earth's surface.

Latitude is the angle between you, the centre of the earth, and the equator. Imagine a line going from you to the centre of the earth. Now imagine a line from the centre of the earth to the point on the equator that is closest to your home. Your latitude is the angle between those two lines. (see 13-1). Can you see how angles of latitude are different at different places around the world? Latitude can be measured using a simple measurement made on a star, the North Star. Navigators over the millennia have used the North Star to find out exactly where they are in relation to the equator and the North pole. So, by calculating your latitude in this way, you will be performing an activity that is about as old as science itself.

The Earth viewed from the side

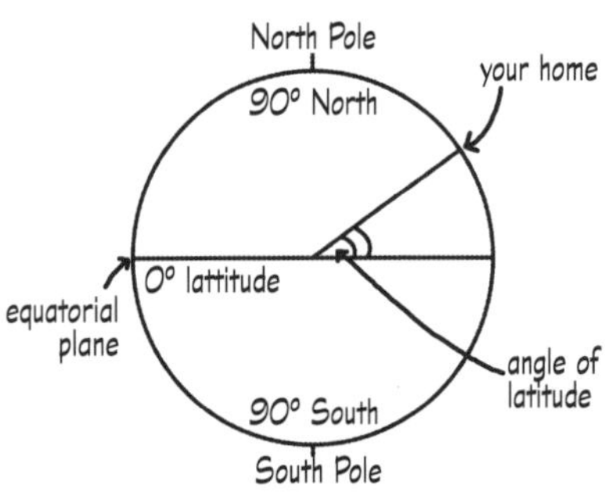

13-1 Latitude

Longitude is the angle between you, the centre of the earth, and the Prime Meridian. The Prime Meridian is an imaginary line that runs from the North pole to the South pole and crosses a British town called Greenwich. Imagine that same line going from you to the centre of the earth. Now imagine a line from the centre of the earth to the point on the Prime Meridian closest to your home.

Your longitude is the angle between those two lines. (see 13-2).

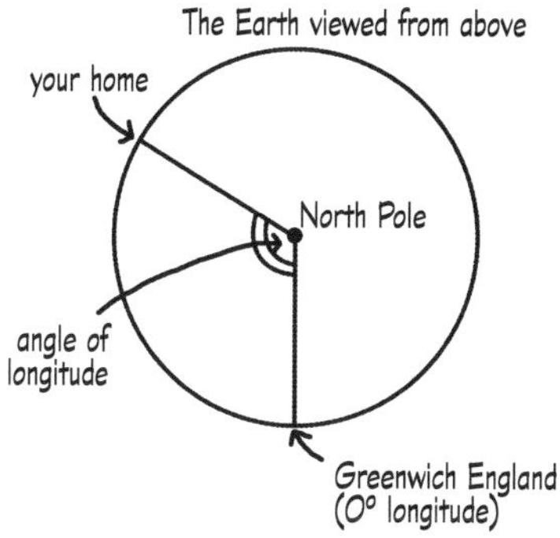

13-2 Longitude

Going Ahead

Finding the latitude of your home

1. Find the North Star on a clear night. You can do this is by first finding the Big Dipper, (see 13-3 The Big Dipper) which is always in the northern sky. If you line up the two stars that form the left-hand side of the dipper, then extend that line upwards along the same path, the first bright star you encounter is the North Star.
2. On a flat deck or porch railing, use the tape and protractor to attach the piece of cardboard so that it is standing vertically. Make sure the cardboard is pointing straight at the North Star and that the end of the cardboard closest to you is flush with the edge of the railing (see 13-4 Finding Your Angle of Latitude).
3. Holding the ruler against the cardboard with one end on the railing, point it towards the North Star. Then use the ruler to draw a line that points straight at the star.
4. Repeat the activity several times using the other pieces of cardboard along the porch railing.

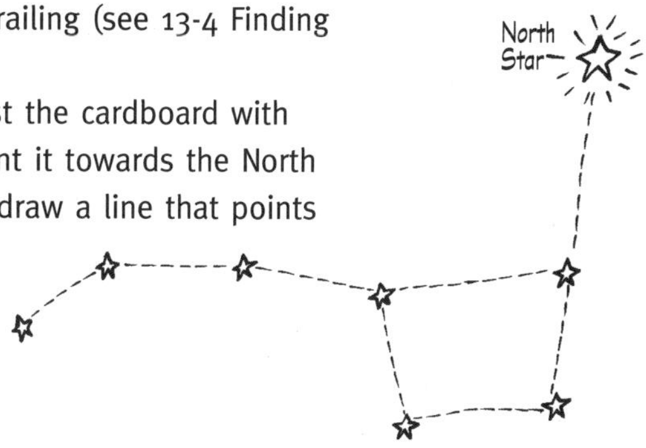

13-3 the Big Dipper

5. Use the protractor to measure the angle between the Earth's surface and the North Star on all the pieces of cardboard. Add the obtained values together and divide by the number of measurements you made to obtain an average measurement. This average will be more accurate than if you had only measured once.
6. The average angle will be the latitude of your hometown. You can compare your measurement

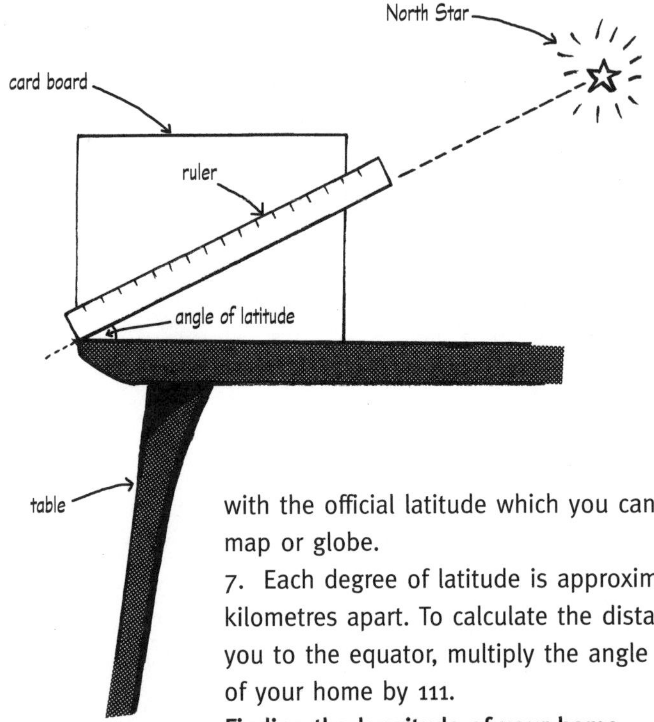

13-4 Finding Your Angle of Latitude

with the official latitude which you can find on a map or globe.

7. Each degree of latitude is approximately 111 kilometres apart. To calculate the distance from you to the equator, multiply the angle of latitude of your home by 111.

Finding the longitude of your home

1. Greenwich is the place we use as our reference point for measuring time and time differences. The time in every time zone in the world is measured in relation to Greenwich Mean Time. A simple way to figure out your longitude is to look at the time difference between your home and Greenwich Mean Time. Every degree of longitude is equivalent to a time difference of 4 minutes. This means that for every degree west of Greenwich, 12 o'clock noon occurs four minutes later. British Columbia is 8 hours behind Greenwich. Eight hours is 8 X 60 minutes, or 480 minutes. Using this information, you can calculate how many degrees west we are of the Prime Meridian. Consult an atlas or globe to check your calculation.

TAKING IT FURTHER

1. Think about your findings:
   - Why does the angle to the North Star equal the angle of latitude? The North Star is located almost directly over the North pole, but millions of miles above so the rays of light from the North Star are always coming towards the Earth from the north (see 13-5 Calculations Using the North Star).

     The angle to the North Star is 'a,' and the angle of latitude is 'c'. Note that since 'a' + 'b' + 90 must be 180 degrees (half of a circle, which is 360 degrees) and 'b' + 90 + 'c' must be 180 degrees (the internal angles of all triangles add up to 180 degrees) then 'a' must equal 'c.' So, when you measure your angle to the North Star, you are also measuring your angle of latitude.

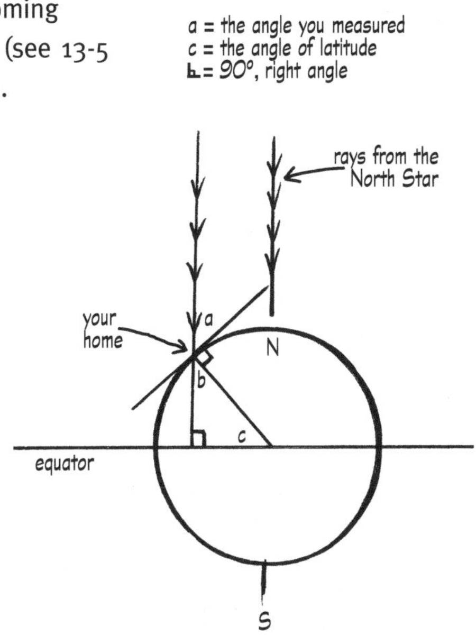

13-5 Calculations Using the North Star

2. Other things to think about:
   - What angle of latitude would your neighbours calculate?
   - What angle would a kid on the equator calculate?
   - How about somebody at the North Pole?
   - Now that you know that the distance between lines of latitude is 111 km, calculate how far it is from the equator to the North Pole.
   - Now calculate how far it is to walk right around the circumference of the Earth.

Resource Connections

- Greenwich Time and the Discovery of the Longitude by Derek Howse
- Latitude and Longitude at Noon: Self-taught by Paul J. Miller

Meet a Scientist

Bethany Foote is a computer scientist.

WHAT DO YOU DO?

I am creating a portion of the software that will be used to control the new robotic arm on the International Space Station. I have also worked on the software for the Mobile Base Station that the arm travels on. The Mobile Base Station attaches to the solar arrays and is basically a cart that moves the arm around. When writing software, I type commands into a file that the computer translates to a language that it can understand. Then the program is run and the computer follows the commands that I typed. Sometimes the program will not behave the way that I expect, so I have to go through the code and figure out where the problem is. This can often take several days.

WHAT MADE YOU WANT TO BE A COMPUTER SCIENTIST?

I like problem solving. I was inspired to work in this field by working with computers in elementary and high school.

TELL US A STORY ABOUT AN EXCITING TIME OR EVENT IN YOUR CAREER.

One of the most exciting events in my career is when Chris Hadfield, the Canadian astronaut, came to visit my project team at work. He told us all about his trip to the Mir space station and what it was like to go on a spacewalk. I was able to get Mr. Hadfield's autograph which I now have hanging in my office.

Animal Behaviour

What's It All About?

In this activity you will observe the behaviour of animals. We've all observed animals, but you will scientifically record what they do and how much time they spend doing it. While some animal behaviour is innate, some is learned. The behaviour component of an animal's characteristics is just as important as its appearance; thus understanding it is key to the needs of various animals in both their natural and human-made habitats. This activity involves careful observation, as well as categorizing and recording animal behaviour for future analysis.

What You Will Need

- A notebook and pencil
- A timer (a watch, stop-watch, or clock will do)
- Sheets of coloured tissue paper
- A pop bottle cap
- Sticky tape
- A bell

Going Ahead

1. Choose an animal in your community that you want to study. Household pets are good subjects to start with. Squirrels, birds, and insects also make interesting subjects.
2. Take a preliminary look at the animal's behaviour and decide what categories of behaviour would make up its daytime activities (see the list below for examples). This doesn't have to be an exhaustive list; you can always expand on it later on.
3. Draw up a chart showing the behaviour categories.
4. Spend some time observing the animal closely. Record the amount of time it spends on each activity. Try to stay at a safe distance from the animal—you don't want to disturb its natural behaviour. Spy on it if possible. Your observations may look like this:
    - "Activity A: 10 seconds. Activity B: 30 seconds. Activity C: 15 seconds. Activity D: 20 seconds," and so on.
5. Enter the activities on the chart. At the end of

the observation period, calculate the total time spent on each activity.

6. Observe the same animal at different times of the day, as well as different seasons. Compare its behaviour with that of other animals.

7. Analyze the observed behaviours to learn more about the particular animal and/or species.

8. Some possible activity categories to guide your analysis could be:

Squirrels:

- resting;
- obtaining food;
- grooming;
- territorial behaviour (chasing, threatening, fighting);
- mating;
- communicating (calling, tail waving, etc.).

Birds:

- resting;
- obtaining food;
- grooming;
- nest building;
- territorial behaviour;
- mating;
- food preferences (see Activity 1—Observing Birds);
- communicating (calling, displaying, posturing).

Cat or dog:

- grooming;
- obtaining food;
- resting;
- aggression;
- territorial behaviour (barking, chasing, etc.);
- mating;
- playing;
- communicating (calling, tail wagging, sniffing).

Bees:

- obtaining food (from flowers);
- travel;
- resting;
- communicating;
- time on flowers of plant (species A, species B, etc);
- time on flower 1;
- time on flower 2, etc;
- time on plant 1, plant 2 of species A;
- time spent within 1 metre radius of a particular plant or object;
- general direction of journey;
- how was the behaviour of a bee influenced by a second bee?

Additional Bee or Wasp Study Activities:

- Make artificial flowers using different coloured paper. Place a pop bottle cap full of sugar water or honey in the middle of one of your paper flowers. Wait for a bee to find it, then time how long it takes for the number of bees to increase to two bees. How long does it take before a third bee finds the sugar water? A fourth? Once the bees have definitely found the water—a lot of them are drinking it—move the sugar cap and mix up the positions of the coloured flowers. Where do the bees go first?

Fish:

- obtaining food;
- resting;
- communicating;
- aggression;
- swimming;
- Place a piece of tape on the side of the tank, then count how many times the fish pass it.
- How long do the fish spend at the bottom,

the middle, and the top of the tank? (Use a piece of tape to divide the tank.)

- Does the time of day affect their behaviour? How do the above times change at different times of the day?
- Does the weather affect their behaviour? How do the above times change in different weather conditions?
- How do activities change in different degrees of lightness or darkness?
- Can the fish anticipate feeding time? Can you prove this with your records? Can you train a fish into a feeding response using a bell?

Taking It Further

1. Observe animal behaviour in other locations. You can try the same types of observations and measurements at the zoo or aquarium.
2. Human beings are animals too. Observe people at the beach or the park. It's important to be sensitive and polite. Staring directly at people will make them feel uncomfortable—try to be inobtrusive and discreet.
3. Try activities 1, 31 and 32 which are also about animal behaviour.

Resource Connections

- *Animals Alive! An Ecological Guide to Animal Activities* by Dennis Holley
- *On Behaviour: Instinct is a Cheshire Cat* by Peter H. Klopfer
- *The Amazing Things Animals Do* by Susan McGrath
- *How Animals Behave* by The National Geographic Society

15 What Dams Do

What's It All About?

Dams play a significant role in the lives of most British Columbians. They occur naturally through the buildup of debris, or artificially through human and animal intervention. Since dams help us with flood control, irrigation, and power generation, they play an important role in our lives; yet most people don't think about dams much at all. Learning about the many scientific components that are involved in the construction and operation of dams can be fascinating and can inspire your children to interests in engineering and nature. This activity involves finding a dam near your home and making observations about its structure, operation and impact on the human community, as well as the community of plants and animals that live nearby. The activity also invites you to experiment with building your own dams.

What You Will Need

- A notebook and pencil
- A map of the area
- Possibly binoculars
- A tray or flat dish

Going Ahead

1. Find a dam close to your home and plan a day trip to go and check it out. If you don't know of any dams, get out a map and check nearby bodies of water for a tell-tale straight edge at one end—this usually indicates the presence of a dam.
2. When you arrive, your first task is to classify your dam. There are two basic types of dams.:

i. Concrete dams (see 15-1 Concrete Dams)

These dams are generally built in deep, narrow valleys where the sides and base of the valley are solid rock. This is because concrete can be more easily attached to rock than to other natural surfaces, and since it's expensive, the less the builders need to use, the better. There are three types of concrete dams:

- Arch dam: From a bird's eye view, you can see that this type of dam is an arched structure designed to curve against the water's flow pattern so that the water flowing towards the dam presses against the outside of the curve. Some arch dams consist of arches in two directions. Arched supporting structures are much stronger than straight ones.

- Gravity dam: The wall of this type of dam leans towards the water, using gravity to resist its force.
- Buttress dam: From a bird's eye view, this type of dam makes a straight line across a river. The buttresses are vertical, wedge-shaped columns built on the dry side to strengthen the dam.

ii. Embankment dams (see 15-2 Embankment Dam)

These dams are built out of piles of rock or soil. Their strength lies in the great weight of the material. Embankment dams are suitable for wider valleys where there is less solid rock along the edges. They tend to leak a bit, so you will usually find a waterproof liner along the water side of the dam.

3. Once you know what type of dam you are observing, you can record your findings and start to look for certain features that will help you figure out how the dam works.

- Spillways allow surplus water past the dam in a controlled way. Do you see a spillway in your dam? Is its size adjustable? How do you think it works?
- If you are observing an embankment dam, look for the liner. What is it made of?
- Are there any buttresses on your dam? If so, how many do you see? Are they purely decorative, or do they have a functional purpose? How can you tell?
- Is there a generating station in the dam?
- Do you see a fish ladder that allows migratory fish to swim past the dam?

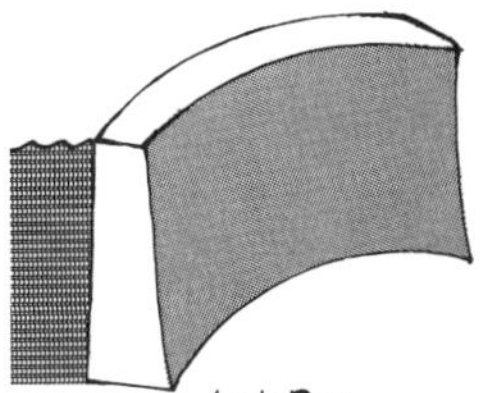

Arch Dam

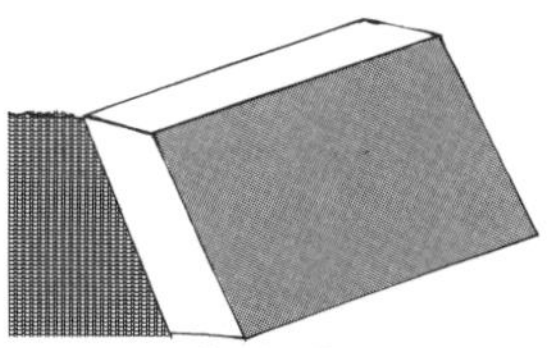

Gravity Dam

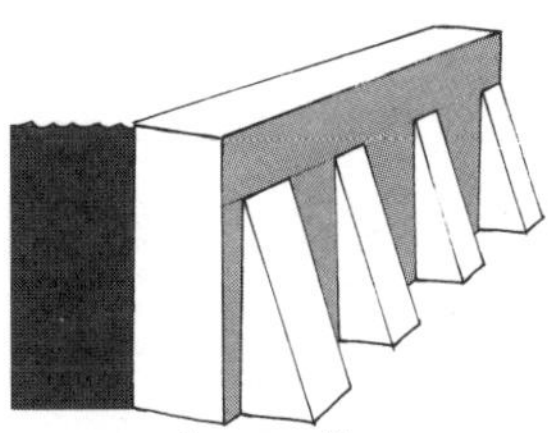

Buttress Dam

15-1 Concrete Dams

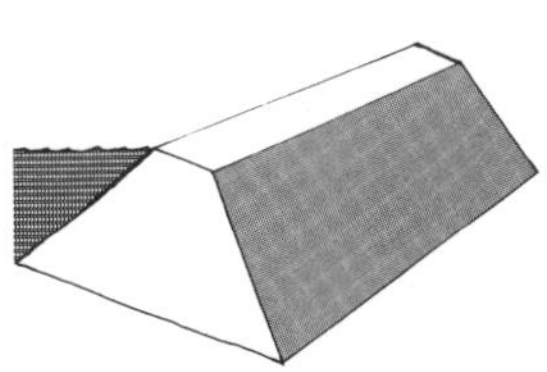

15-2 Embankment Dam

- How many people do you see working on the dam? What jobs are they doing?
- Do you see roads along the top of the dam? What purpose do they serve?
- Is the shape and style of the dam attractive?

4. Many dams have information about them posted nearby for public display. This information will supplement the facts you have collected and will help you consider these questions:

- Why do you think your dam was built? Look for evidence of what purpose it serves.

  a. Does it prevent floods?

  b. Does it create a drinking water reservoir? Are there any pumping stations on the water side? Looking at your map, see if you can find the location of the water catchment area (the river systems that provide the water for the lake behind the dam).

  c. Does it generate electricity? Look for generating stations and hydro wires. Think about how many people live in the community serviced by the dam. What are their energy requirements?

  d. Does it create an irrigation lake? Look for channels or pipes that emerge from the dam. Again, think about the community around it—are farming and crop irrigation important community issues?

  e. Does it create a lake for leisure activities (boating, fishing and swimming)? Is this the primary purpose of the dam or a spin-off feature?
- What impact does your dam have on the surrounding community?

  a. the human population?

  b. the fish in the original river?

  c. the plants and animals in the vicinity, including trees?

- Have any non-native animals or plants been introduced into the lake behind the dam? If so, think about whether this was deliberate or accidental.
- Which towns obtain water from the dam?
- Which towns derive electricity from the dam (if any)?

Taking It Further

1. In the middle of an old tray or flat dish, build an embankment dam of dirt or sand. Pour water on one side, and time how long it takes for the water to get past the dam and reach the same level on both sides. Add a liner of plastic sheet or aluminum foil, and repeat the experiment. Compare your times. Try to make a perfect seal using realistic materials.
2. Try to make a model of a concrete dam using old pieces of wood or plastic. Try to fit these as snugly as possible into your tray or dish, and then pour the water in on one side. What kind of problems do you encounter? One of the most significant problems will probably be water getting around or under the dam. This is a problem in real dams too. Real dams on soft valley bottoms have a 'cut-off' of clay or rocks reaching into the earth to stop water from bypassing the dam and eroding its structure.
3. If you have access to a stream, try to build a dam to block the flow of the water. Think about what problems you might encounter. What will happen when the water starts to accumulate behind the dam? Will it start to pool up, or will it push its way past the dam and carry on downstream? Can you find a way to contain it so that your dam will remain intact as the force of the water builds up behind it? Don't forget to always break it up afterwards, so that your experiment has minimal impact

on the environment. Another good place to experiment with building dams is on a beach crossed by a stream.

4. Animals are engineers too. Beavers are excellent dam builders. On hikes, look for beaver dams (generally messy piles of wooden fragments at the end of a swampy lake). Their dams form a lake in which the beaver can hunt for food. Do some reading about beaver dams and think about how their dams are similar and different from the human-made dams you have been studying.

5. Dams were one of the first communal structures to be built by humans. Their construction played a role in the development of communities as we know them today. How do you think dams promoted the development of social order, cities and communities?

6. Historically, dams were primarily used for flood control and irrigation. The technologies used for power generation have changed. Initially we used water wheels driven by water running down specially-constructed channels that were often at the side of a dam. Are there any old water wheels in your community that you could study?

7. Today, after thousands of years of dam construction, the ethics of dam building are being examined. To understand why, consider the good that dams can do, and compare it with the damage associated with barricading a river or waterway. What value is associated with the creation of a new lake? What dangers are associated with this? If rivers above and below a dam change their patterns, what happens to people living above and below a dam site? How does dam construction affect them and their community?

8. Do some reading on fish migration and learn more about how fish ladders work.

Resource Connections

- *Dams* by Neil Ardley
- *Dams* by Cass R. Sandak
- http://www.bchydro.com/education

Where the Buildings Are

an introduction to community planning

What's It All About?

Buildings are an important part of your community's structure, and knowing the types of buildings, their presence and their locations is an important part of community awareness. To a geographer, this is the study of urban planning and design. In this activity, you will categorize building types, researching their locations on a city map. You will be introduced to map-reading and map-making skills as well as compass orientation.

Going Ahead

1. Go through the following list of building types. Can you think of some nearby examples of these buildings?

Houses:

- one level (bungalow)
- 2 or 3 levels
- farmhouse
- mansion

Apartments:

- low rise (2-4 levels)
- high rise (more than 4)
- townhouse (side-by-side)

Shops:

- single level
- under apartments or offices
- department store
- super (mega) store
- mall

Office building:

- low rise
- high rise

Factories:

- small
- large

What You Will Need

- A notebook and pencil
- A city map or a map of your surrounding area
- Large sheets of paper or cardboard
- A ruler
- A protractor
- Possibly a compass

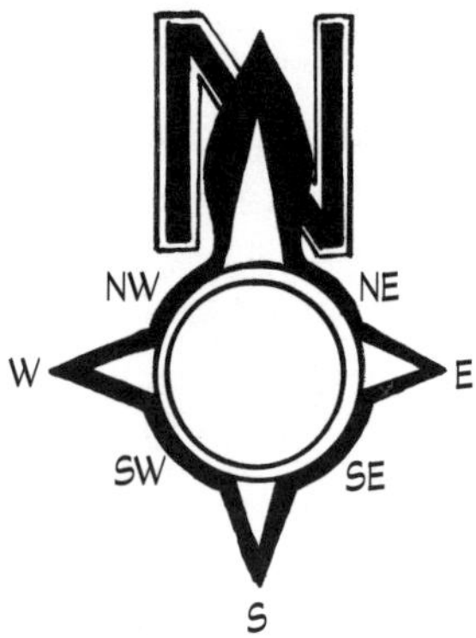

6-1 Compass Star

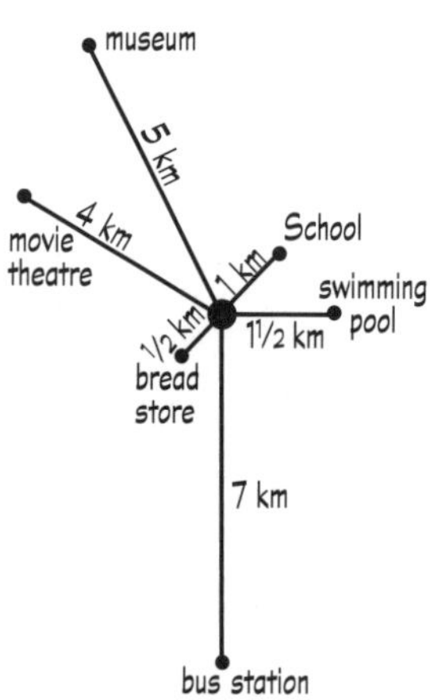

6-2 Starburst Map

Accomodation:

- motel
- hotel
- guesthouse/bed and breakfast

transportation:

- parking lot on ground level
- multilevel parking lot
- bus station
- train station
- airport
- gas station

entertainment/culture:

- bowling alley
- movie theatre (single or multiplex)
- theatre (for drama)
- concert hall (for music)
- club
- ice rink
- golf course/clubhouse
- stadium
- museum
- art gallery
- swimming pool
- video arcade
- community centre

religion

- church
- synagogue
- mosque
- temple

2. Locate the nearest examples on the city map.
3. Using the map, measure the distance from your home to each building.
4. Convert the distances to kilometres using the map key.
5. On a large sheet of paper, mark your home in the centre and label it.

6. Orient the paper—North should be at the top of the sheet—and draw a compass star (see 16-1 Compass Star).
7. Draw the approximate location of each building type. Using a straight line, connect each building type to your home. Indicate the distance and compass direction. (By the end, the map should look like a starburst with your house at the centre—see 16-2.)

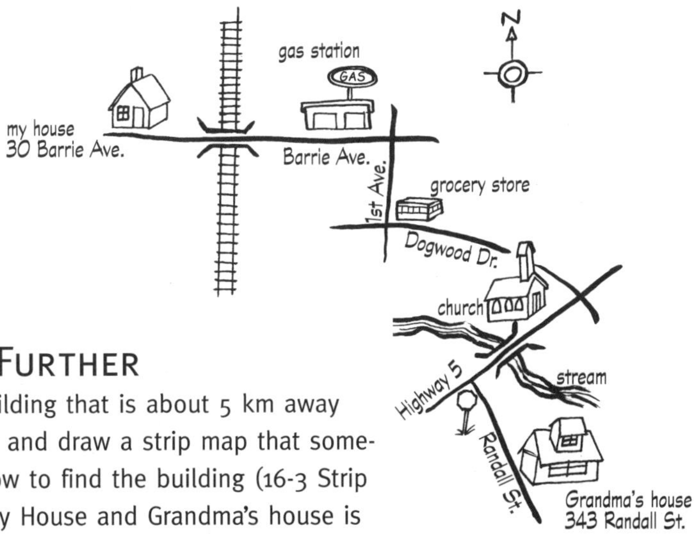

16-3 Strip Map Between My House and Grandma's house

Taking It Further

1. Choose a building that is about 5 km away from your home and draw a strip map that somebody could follow to find the building (16-3 Strip Map Between My House and Grandma's house is an example of this type of map). Show your route as a single wavy line, with important landmarks and intersections marked along the way.
2. Design a utopia—your idea of a perfect town—with everything you like and need and the most efficient locations. Make sure you include a good selection of items from the above list.
3. Design a building that improves on one you have recently visited. For example, if a parking lot seems poorly laid out, redesign it to solve the problems you noticed.
4. Design the perfect public transportation system for your area. Make sure all the buildings on your map are well served.

Resource Connections

- Cities 2000 by Robert Royston

17 Getting to Know BC's Top Mosses

What's It All About?

Mosses are small green plants found in many habitats in BC. This province has one of the richest assortments of mosses of the non-tropical zones of the Earth. Thus, moss biodiversity in BC is higher than in most other temperate parts of the planet.

What You Will Need

- A notebook and pencil
- A magnifying lens
- Possibly a moss identification book

Mosses are delicate and fascinating plants. They produce no flowers, but reproduce through the dispersal of spores, which are produced on a slender stalk—called the sporophyte—that sticks up out of the green mass of the moss. At the end of the stalk is a swollen tip—called the capsule—that actually produces the spores.

Mosses are homes for many small animals that help to maintain the balance of our natural ecosystems. It is important to understand mosses in order to develop an appreciation of ecological diversity and the uniqueness of BC's nature. In this activity, you will hunt for some of the most common and interesting mosses in the province.

Going Ahead

1. If you have a mossy lawn, this is a good place to start collecting samples. The moss you will find is most likely the star moss—*Rhytidiadelphus squarrosus*, pronounced 'rye-tiddy-a-delfus skwar-osus'. Its leaves stick out from the stem at right angles, giving this moss a prickly, star-shaped appearance when viewed from above (see 17-1 *Rhyitidiadelphus squarrosus*).

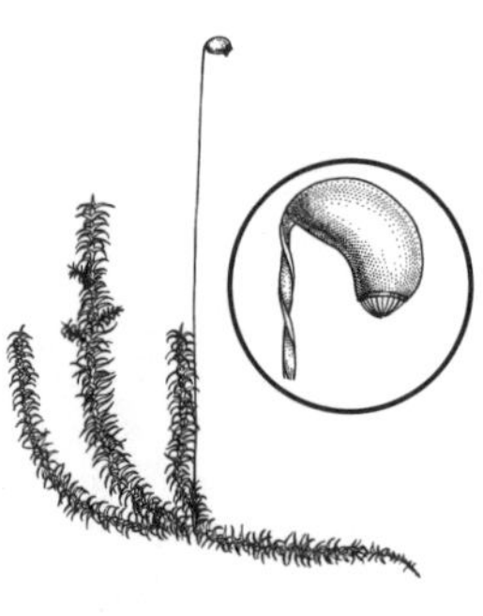

17-1 *Rhyitidiadelphus squarrosus*

2. Collect samples of some other common moss you may find in a local forest or natural space; they are all pretty easy to identify. The following five moses are common enough that it's acceptable to pick a small specimen and take it home to draw or study more closely. Compare each of the

descriptions with the illustrations (17-2 Other Common Mosses).

- The hair cap moss (*Polytrichum juniperinum*) is found on forest floors and logs. It is an erect, stiff plant with leaves 4-8 mm long flaring out from the stem. Its capsule looks squarish when cut across the middle. When young, the capsule has a hairy cap on it; when old, a whitish membrane covers the mouth of the capsule.
- The step moss (*Hylocomium splendens*) is found in carpets in the forest. It has reddish stems and tiny leaves. Its most identifiable feature is the new branch that it puts out each year. Together these branches are reminiscent of steps.
- Some peat moss (Sphagnum species) are found in bogs, contributing to peat production. But not all peat mosses are bog-lovers. The best way to identify them is by the looking at the stem. Peat mosses generally have a head of branches at the end of the stem, and tufts along the stem. Each tuft has some branches flaring out and some hanging down against the stem.
- The cord moss (*Funaria hygrometrica*) grows on disturbed sites, especially old bonfire sites. The plant is small, light green and bulb-like. The stalks of the sporophytes are wiry and yellow, twisting into different shapes when the moisture in the air changes. Capsules are pear-shaped and grooved, while the teeth around the mouth are reddish.
- The broom moss or cranesbill moss (*Dicranum scoparium*) is found on tree bases, humus (decaying plant material) and logs. The capsule is shaped like a bird's head with

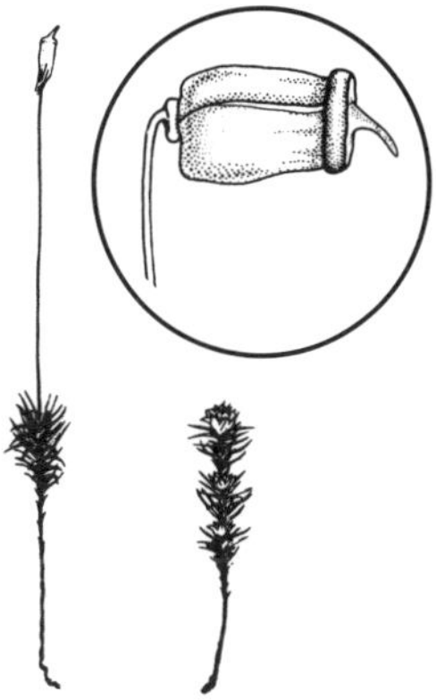

Polytrichum juniperinum

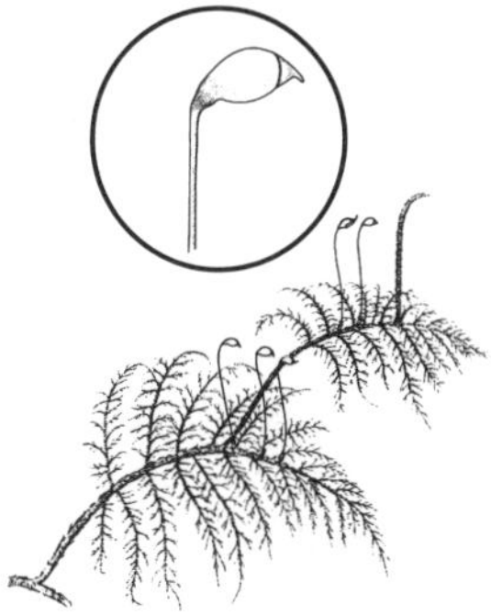

Hylocomium splendens

Sphagnum

17-2 Other Common Mosses

a long beak. The leaves are long, C-shaped and they all point in one direction.

3. Draw the samples of mosses you have collected, and try to identify them using a moss book.

4. Keep a log recording where you find each type of moss. Many mosses have preferred habitats, making identification easier. Try to define their preferred habitats.

Taking It Further

1. Construct a small terrarium using the various mosses you find. Remember to spray them once a week to keep them moist.

2. Take close-up photographs of these small plant jewels.

3. Begin to look at moss forests very closely (yes, you need to get your nose to the ground). Find out what animals inhabit these mossy environments and learn more about their behaviour and life styles.

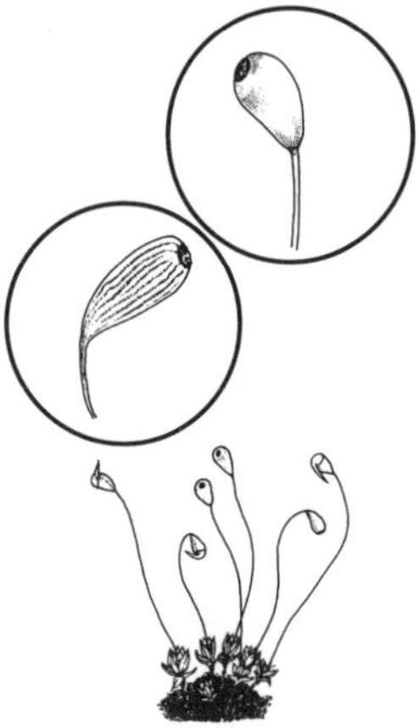

Funaria hygrometrica

Dicranum scoparium

17-2 Other Common Mosses

Resource Connections

- Some Mosses of British Columbia by W.B. Schofield
- Mosses and Lichens of the Pacific Northwest by D.H. Vitt, J.E. Marsh and R.B. Bovey

**Thanks to Dr. Wilf Schofield (UBC Botany Department) for permission to reproduce his drawings.*

Bridge Engineering

What's It All About?

Bridges are prominent and easily-examined examples of the application of engineering principles. Bridge-building requires very careful planning and skillful construction to ensure that the structure can span a gap. In this activity, you will examine a bridge in your local community and evaluate its category of design. You will then test the efficiency of the bridge design by building a model. This foray into basic engineering will introduce you to the scientific principles engineers must consider when designing and building bridges.

Going Ahead

What You Will Need

- A notebook and pencil
- A city or area map
- Some drinking straws, bamboo skewers, popsicle sticks or spaghetti
- A piece of cardboard
- Masking tape
- Some straight pins and paper clips

1. Locate and visit a bridge close to your home and sketch it.
2. Estimate the bridge's length by pacing it. Then measure the length of your pace and multiply the length of your pace by the number of paces you took. You could also drive across the bridge and use the car's odometer to measure distance. To estimate the height, use one of the methods described for measuring trees (see Activity 5—Tree Charting).
3. Deduce why the bridge was built. How would you get to the other side if there was no bridge? How many kilometers would the detour be? Find out when the bridge was constructed. (The date of construction is often posted on the bridge.) Using a city map, decide if there could have been an alternative location in which to build this bridge, and visit the site to assess its pros and cons.
5. Classify your bridge (see 18-1 Types of Bridges).
   - A beam bridge has a straight rigid piece of material, called a beam, spanning the two sides. Try to determine the basis of the beam's rigidity. What engineering principles have been used to make it rigid? Look for trusses which

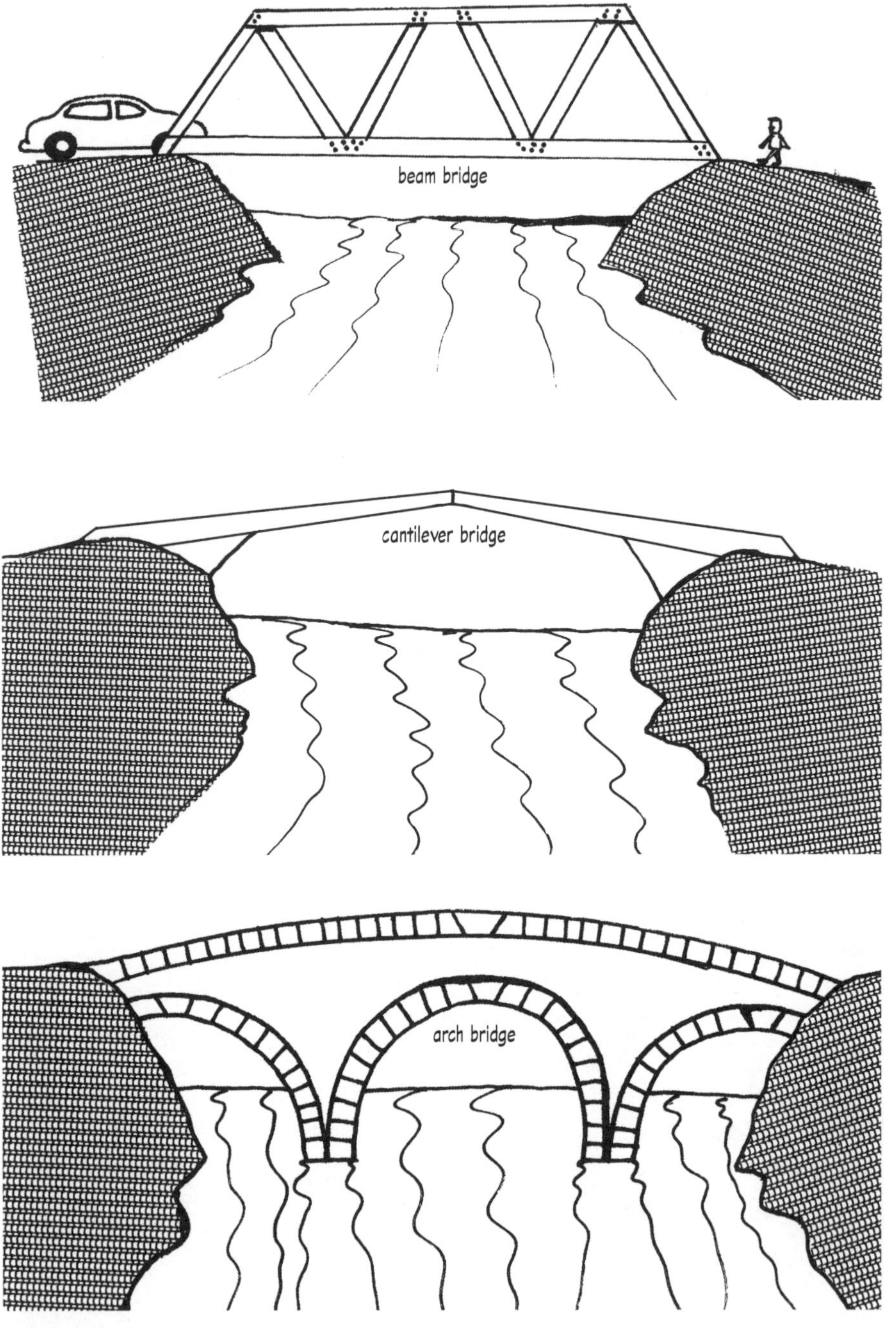

8-1 Types of Bridges

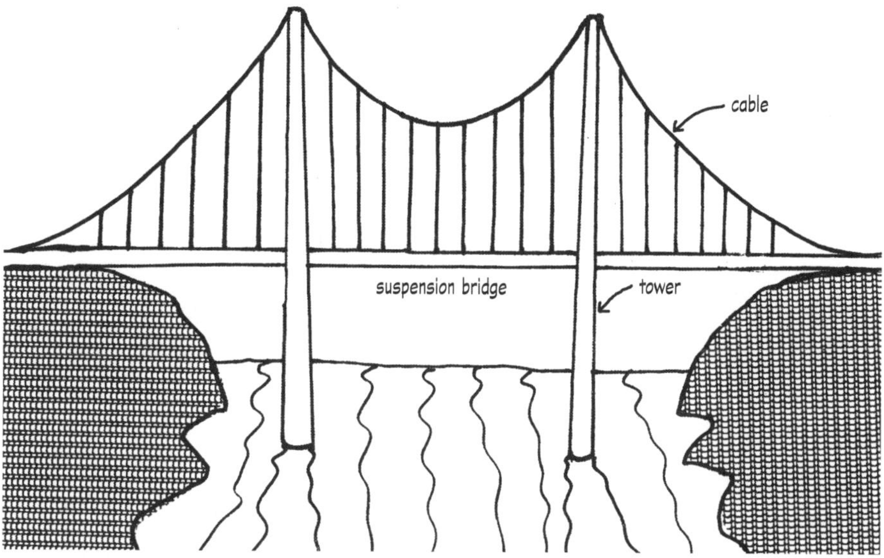

8-1 Types of Bridges

are made up of triangles attached together to make a beam. Triangular structures are strong, light and resist bending. Trusses derive their strength from their component triangles.

- A cantilever bridge is built with both ends firmly attached to each bank. The bridge decks jut out and meet in the middle.
- An arch bridge resembles an inverted U shape. An arch is an efficient and elegant load-bearing structure.
- A suspension bridge hangs from an overhead cable that is anchored to the ground at each end and supported by towers.

6. How many spans are there? Look for piers in the middle, and abutments on the banks. Trestle bridges are beam bridges that derive all of their strength from multiple supports (piers) which are composed of triangles that are created by cross bracing.
7. What is the bridge made of? wood? steel? concrete? stone? What do you think determined the choice of material? What are the advantages of each?

8. What problems had to be overcome to build the bridge? (Take into consideration when the bridge was built).
9. How do you think the bridge was built? The Granville Street Bridge in Vancouver was built by cantilevering out from each side and meeting in the middle. What was the first thing done in the case of your bridge? The second? How many different types of skilled workers were needed?
10. Take a critical look at your bridge. Is it a pleasing design? Does it 'fit in' with the surroundings? Has the bridge created any problems for the community? Could these have been foreseen? Should it be replaced or widened? How could that be achieved?
11. How could the bridge be improved? Does it accommodate different types of travel (i.e. foot, bike, car, train)? Bridges are meant to bridge a gap, so if any of these forms of travel are difficult, redesign the bridge to accommodate that mode of travel. (Keep in mind that you should not make the other forms of travel more difficult).

Taking It Further

1. Visit another bridge with a different design. Compare and contrast your two bridges.
2. Make a model of your first bridge using simple household materials. Spaghetti, popsicle sticks, drinking straws, bamboo skewers and cardboard make useful building materials. Straight pins and paper clips are good connecting tools. Experiment with assorted materials to reinforce structural strength and stability. Test the strength and stability of your bridge by gradually placing a number of rocks or other weights on the bridge deck.
3. Could the bridge be made stronger using the same materials but with a different design?

Resource Connections

- How Bridges are Made by Jeremy Kingston
- Bridges by Kate Petty and Terry Cash
- The Guiness Book of Structures: Bridges, Towers, Tunnels and Dams... by John H. Stephens
- Structures: The Way Things are Built by Nigel Hawkes

Meet a Scientist

Alfred Kao is a bridge engineer

What do you do?

I use my knowledge of science and engineering to plan, design, build and repair bridges. Some of the bridges I have worked on include the No. 2 Road Bridge in Richmond, the Broadway Bridge in Vancouver, and the Trent River Bridge near Courtenay (on Vancouver Island). Bridges carry cars, people, utilities or any combination of these, across rivers, canyons or roads. When we are contracted to design a bridge, we are told how much the bridge has to carry and how far it has to span. Bridges that span shorter distances are usually built from concrete or steel beams. Bridges that span longer distances are usually hung from cables or supported on arches. Bridges with a shorter span are usually less expensive to build than longer bridges. We sometimes make a long span from several short spans by adding support columns to the bridge. Bridges that cross a waterway used by large ships, such as the Lion's Gate Bridge, have to have a long span. Keeping in mind that the bridge can't cost too much, we need to consider the type of soil the bridge will be built on, the impact of construction on the environment and the bridge's overall appearance.

What made you want to be a bridge engineer?

I enjoy creating new structures. My father was a bridge engineer and encouraged me to study science because it would give me a lot of career choices. I chose to become an engineer because it would allow me to apply what I've learned about science and mathematics to create things which improve people's quality of life.

Tell us a story about an exciting time or event in your career.

The most exciting time in my career was working on the No. 2 Road Bridge in Richmond. Under the direction of other senior engineers, I was given the opportunity to work on all parts of the project, including planning the type of bridge, designing the details of the structure and supervising its construction. It was an opportunity to create something new—a new route used by many people to ease their travel to work or to the airport. For me, this was the reason I went into engineering.

Snail Population Biology

What's It All About?

In this activity you will take a new look at snails by examining their unique habits. You will learn about basic population biology and biological diversity through analyses of snail populations and assessments of the snails' variations.

Going Ahead

What You Will Need

- A notebook and pencil
- Several plastic tubs and lids with small holes for air
- A one-litre plastic pop bottle
- Sticky tape
- A marking pen
- Several small pots of hobby paint (enamel or acrylic) or coloured nail polish

1. Determining distribution.

Look for snails in your neighbourhood. Snails come out mainly at night—you'll need to use a flashlight—or in the daytime after a rain storm. Look for them on the branches of bushes, trees and other plants, as well as in long grass, where they often hide. Be systematic while collecting. Record the number and types of snails you find in each site (e.g. each bush). Draw a map of the collection site and use it to record where you found the snails.

2. Estimating population size.

After drying the shells with a cloth, mark them with a dot or a number, using coloured paint (see 19-1 Marking Snails). Make you sure you paint away from the shell opening. Let the paint dry—use the kind that dries quickly—and release the snails randomly over the area. Record the point of release.

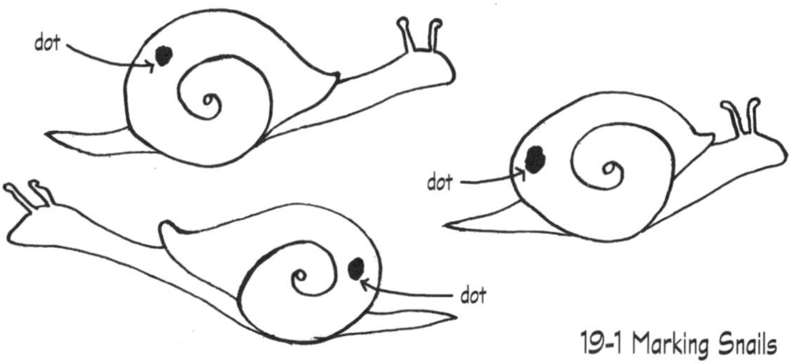

19-1 Marking Snails

A week later, collect the same number of snails. If you find any of the marked snails, record their location and compare it with the previous one. The aim is to see if the snails return to a specific site.

You can estimate the snails' total population size in an area by looking at the proportion of marked snails in your second collection. If you find that 1/3 of the snails you collect are marked, then the total population is

- collection sample size (say 20) x 3 = 60

This is called a mark and recapture experiment, a procedure used extensively in population biology.

3. Finally, write a short summary of your studies on the total population size, site preferences, and mobility of snails.

4. Ask your neighbours if they have seen any marked snails. How far do you think the snails move?

Taking It Further

1. Make a snail habitat in a bottle (see 19-2 A Snail Habitat Bottle).

19-2 A Snail Habitat Bottle

Cut a door into the side of a two litre plastic bottle, using a knife. Try to make the environment inside the bottle as close as possible to the snails' natural environment.

Place five snails inside the bottle and tape the door closed (see 19-3 Snail Habitat). Place the snail bottle somewhere shady—not indoors, though—and record the snails' activities. Place pieces of vegetable in the bottle (carrots, lettuce, potato, etc.) and observe. Describe how snails eat. Record which vegetables they prefer.

2. Do you see different shell patterns or colours on different snails? You are probably looking at

19-3 Snail Habitat

the snail Cepaea (pronounced 'see-pay-a'). These patterns are genetically determined, and confer a type of camouflage that protects snails against predators, mainly birds. Specific patterns provide protection in specific habitats. Test this idea by measuring the proportion of specific patterns collected in different habitats (e.g. reeds, grass, shrubs, etc.). Do the patterns differ?

4. Watch snails in action to learn about how they move. Measure their speed by marking where they are when they start moving, then time them for two minutes and measure the distance covered.

- Distance covered (millimetres) / time (minutes) = distance per minute = speed

Do this on different days when the air temperature is different and look for any correlation between speed and temperature. You can have snail races to find the individual speed record holder (they love to crawl upwards, so position them at the bottom of a vertically-tilted sheet of plastic or piece of wood). Put the snails on their backs and record how long it takes for them to flip over. Are the fastest flippers also the fastest crawlers?

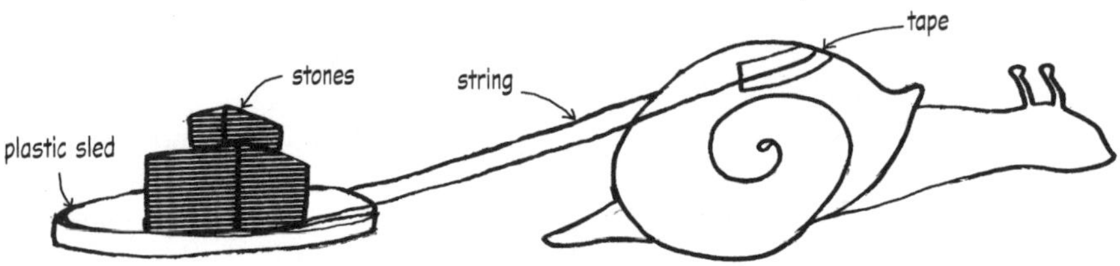

19-4 Measuring Snail Strength

5. Can snails crawl over sharp objects? Try using broken egg shells and razor edges. Get a small wooden block. Ask your parents to tack razor blades around the edge to make an enclosure. Place the snails in the middle and watch what they do.

6. To establish how strong snails are, devise a sled out of a plastic lid and attach it to the shell with tape (see 19-4 Measuring Snail Strength). Add small stones one at a time to the sled. Measure the maximum weight a snail can pull. Weigh the stones to get a precise measure. Find the strongest snail.

7. Place an upside-down flower pot outside and prop it up a bit with a stone, so that snails can get in. Snails go out and eat mainly at night, and will find a hiding place before daytime. Check to see if snails have used your hiding place. Mark them with numbers and put them back in the pot. Check again the next morning to see if you have the same or different snails. Explain the results.

Resource Connections

- Snails by Enid Fisher
- Snails and Slugs by Chris Henwood

A Global Sundial

What's It All About?

A sundial is an instrument that allows you to tell time using the sun. A global sundial is quite different from a normal sundial. It is constructed using a spherical object rather than a flat plate. With a global sundial, you can tell where on the Earth the sun is rising, where it is setting and where it is directly overhead (where it is noon).

As the sun moves across the sky, the shadows cast by trees and buildings change their positions. So do the shadows on a sundial; it is from the positions of these shadows on the dial that you can figure out the time.

When the sun is located in an imaginary plane that goes from north to south and passes directly overhead, a sundial will cast the shortest shadow of the day. It will be noon in apparent solar time at the location of the sundial. At other locations on the Earth's surface however, the time will be different. In some places the sun will just be rising, in others it will be setting and in other places it will be night-time.

In this activity you will learn how to construct a global sundial.

What You Will Need

- A world globe
- A large empty flower pot
- A small piece of plasticene
- A toothpick
- A small piece of cardboard
- A compass

Going Ahead

1. Remove the globe from its stand. Place it on an empty flower pot and stick the piece of plasticene on the city or town where you live. Then place the toothpick in the plasticene at a right angle. Position the globe so that your city is sitting right on top with the toothpick pointing straight up. Make sure light falls directly on your globe, otherwise you won't have a good sundial.
2. Aim the north pole of the globe so that it points to true north (see 20-1 Global Sundial). If you are not sure where north is, you can find it

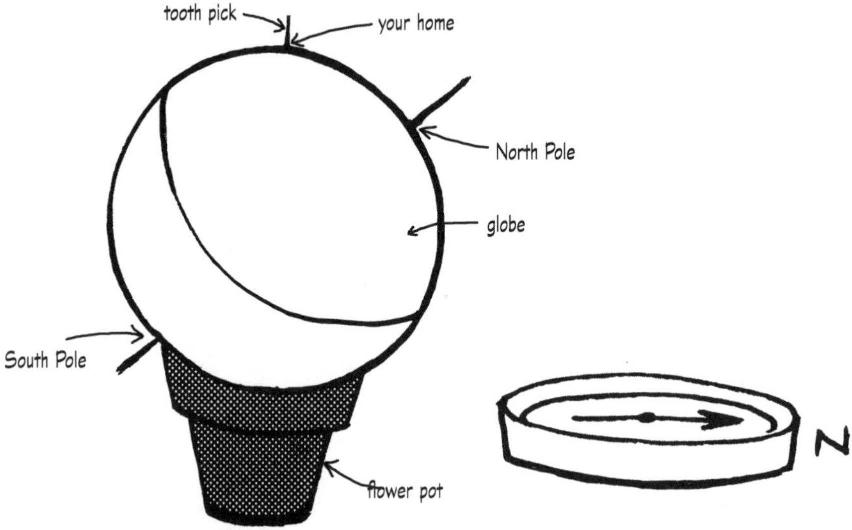

20-1 Global Sundial

with a magnetic compass. The compass needle will point towards magnetic north. In British Columbia, true north is about 20 degrees to the west of magnetic north. The angle between true north and magnetic north is called the magnetic declination. Its actual value varies from location to location, but a 20 degree allowance is close enough. You can find the actual value for your location if you have a topographic map of the place where you live—the magnetic declination will be in the margin of the map.

3. When your location on the globe points upwards and the globe's north pole is aimed towards true north, then the globe is oriented exactly the same way as the earth itself. 'Up' on the earth will be 'up' on the globe, and the north pole of the earth will match the north pole of the globe. The sunlight hitting your globe will fall as it does on the Earth. As a result, you will see

where on the Earth the sun is rising or setting—just look on your globe and see where the line of the shadow falls.

4. You can use your sundial to see where sunrise, sunset, and local noon are throughout the day. Sunrise and sunset can be followed by recording the location of the edges of the shadow that marks the division between day and night on the globe. To find local noon, a small additional piece of apparatus is needed; you can make it out of some cardboard.

- Cut out two small pieces of cardboard of the shape shown in 20-2 Sun Stand.
- Fasten these two pieces so that they stand on their own. You can hold this stand so that the legs rest on the globe. When sunlight is shining on your globe, your sun stand will cast a shadow. As you move the stand around you will find one place where the shadow falls directly beneath the stand. At this location on the globe, the sun is directly overhead, just as it is on the Earth. It is noon at that location and anywhere along the line that includes that point, and the north and south poles (that line of longitude).
- You can also use the little plastic tripods that come in the middle of delivered pizzas. Poke a small hole in the middle and place the tripod on the globe. When the light coming through the hole is exactly in the middle of the tripod's shadow, the sun is directly overhead.

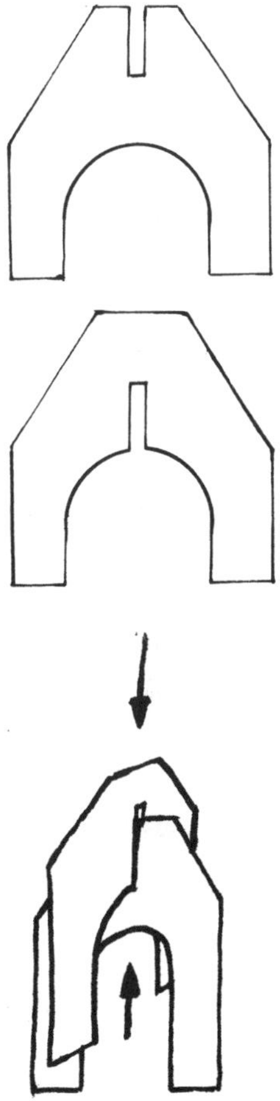

20-2 Sun Stand

Taking It Further

1. Just as observations can be recorded over a day, they can also be made over a longer period of time. For example, if the global sundial is first set up in the winter, you will see that much of the Arctic is in darkness, whereas Antarctica—if it isn't blocked out by the flower pot—will receive continual sunlight. As the seasons progress, the location where the sun is directly overhead will gradually move northwards. At the spring equinox the sun will be directly above the equator. Careful use of your cardboard stand will show this. As spring changes to summer the overhead position of the sun will continue to move northward. On the summer solstice (June 21st), it will be directly above the Tropic of Cancer. The parts of the globe north of 66.5 degrees North latitude (the Arctic Circle) will have continual daylight.
2. Many towns have amateur astronomers who would could assist you in your understanding of sundials and astronomy in general.
3. Try Activity 27- Meet Spaceship Earth, which uses the global sundial for calculating measurements of the Earth.

Resource Connections

- The Observer's Handbook edited by Roy Bishop
- The Amateur Scientist by C.L. Strong
- Sundials: Their Theory and Construction by Albert E. Waugh
- www.rasc.ca (Royal Astronomical Society of Canada)

Monkey Mapping

What's It All About?

The monkeys in this activity are monkey puzzle trees. This unusual tree—its original name is *Araucaria araucana*—is a native of Chile and Argentina. It is related to the Norfolk Island Pine, a houseplant that is sometimes used as a Christmas tree. Monkey puzzle trees were very popular in the 1920s and 1930s, and during those years they were planted in cities and towns throughout BC. Because their leaves are sharp and tough, monkey trees are said to be the only tree that a monkey cannot climb.

In this activity, your challenge will be to find all the monkey trees in town and place them on a map. By now they have grown very big, so they are easy to spot. You will require plant identification and map reading skills, as well as a good sense of direction.

Going Ahead

1. Find a picture of a monkey puzzle tree in a book or on a website. What are its unique features? Find out the conditions in which these trees grow best.
2. Discuss with your family the possible locations of these trees. Whenever you walk, cycle, or drive around town, look for monkey puzzle trees. When you see them, record where they are on your map. Number each tree in your notebook, showing its street and block address. If possible, look at each tree and decide if it is male or female. The males are recognized by their oval-shaped cones that are about 15 cm long. Female cones are round and quite large—almost basket ball-sized. Females are less common.
3. Once you know you have seen most of the specimens, examine the distribution on the map and come up with ideas to explain it.

What You Will Need

- A notebook and pencil
- A city map
- A brightly coloured felt pen

Taking It Further

1. Research the plant in the library and on the Internet.
   - What is its native habitat?
   - What is the range of climates it can withstand?
   - Can it grow anywhere in Canada?
   - Are there any natural predators or diseases that threaten the tree?
2. At the library, research the development of neighbourhoods in your town.
   - How does distribution of the monkey puzzle tree sites correspond with the decades during which different neighbourhoods were developed?
3. Ask someone who works at your local plant store if it is possible to buy a monkey puzzle tree. Would they be desirable trees to have? Find out what problems they present. If you find a female, find out if it produces any seeds. If so, ask if you can collect some. Then try to germinate them and grow your own monkey puzzles.
4. Some other plants that have separate sexes are hollies and forsythias which are not native to Canada, and indian plums (Osmaronia) which is native. Check for these in your neighbourhood and find out which plants are males and females. Take hollies for example: the plants bearing the red berries are females, while the males don't produce any berries.

Resource Connections

- Trees of Vancouver by Gerald S. Straley
- http://www.botany.com/araucaria.html

Wood Frame Construction

why your house doesn't fall down

What's It All About?

In this activity you will learn the engineering principles that enable houses to be built out of wood, a relatively inexpensive, local material. You will also learn how houses are constructed in BC.

Houses are built out of whatever materials are the cheapest, most convenient and compatible with local weather conditions. In central and eastern Canada, many houses were originally built out of stone or brick, but those houses are rare in our province.

British Columbia's forests provided an ample supply of wood, so early houses were built out of wooden logs, which are strong and require relatively little processing. Logs don't come in standard sizes, however, and they are heavy and difficult to manoever. Builders soon developed the wood frame construction method. The lumber industry uses the Imperial system of measurement so some measurements in this activity are in inches and feet.

Frame houses are built one floor at a time using modular components, most often two inch by four inch (2 x 4) cross-section wooden studs nailed into the shape of a cage or frame structure (see 22-1 Frame Structure). Four by eight feet (4 x 8) plywood sheets are then nailed on top, locking the studs in position and making the walls resistant to lateral movement. Laid ceiling joists—usually 2x10 or

What You Will Need

- Corrugated cardboard
- Sticky tape
- Hobby glue or white glue

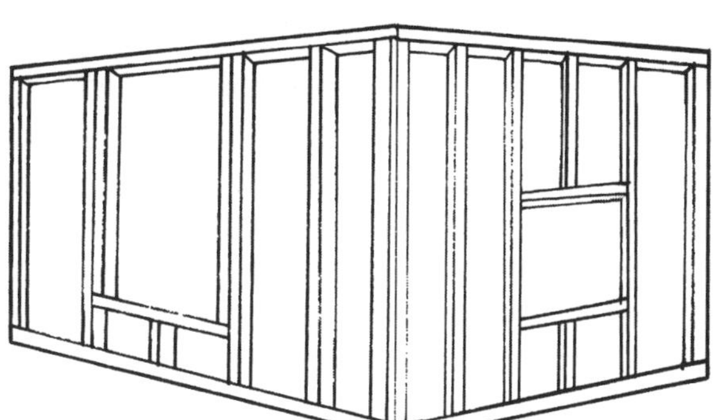

22-1 Frame Structure

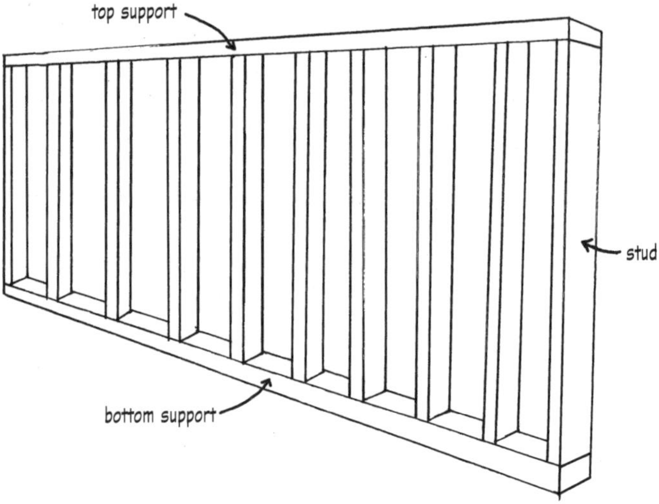

22-2 Stud Frame

2x12—sit across the top of this structure and a layer of plywood is nailed onto them. Thus the first floor is a rigid wooden box. The second floor is built on top and in the same way.

Going Ahead

1. Making a model of a wall.

Cut 12 pieces of cardboard 1 cm x 15 cm. They represent the studs. Then glue or tape them together, using one for the top support and one for the bottom. This is called a stud frame (see 22-2 Stud Frame).

Test your structure's ability to be distorted in three ways (see 22-3 Testing for Distortion):

- twisting;
- collapsing;
- compressing.

Cut two pieces of cardboard 15 cm x 15 cm, to represent plywood. Test these pieces of cardboard for twisting, collapsing, and compressing.

Glue these pieces to your cardboard stud frame to make a wall. Once again, assess the structure's ability to be distorted. You'll find that the structure has become much more rigid. Essentially, you have made a series of I-beams (see 22-4 Cross-section of a Wall). These beams are used extensively in the construction of large buildings like office buildings that are built out of steel and concrete. They are strong and relatively light.

2. Make a model house using the box principle.

Cut 13 pieces of 10 x 10 cm cardboard. Take any piece and check its ability to be bent, twisted, or wobbled.

Make one floor of the house by gluing together 5 pieces (see 22-5 Model House). Then make the second floor and glue it to the first.

Take the remaining three pieces and glue them into a triangular tube. Triangles are extremely resistant to distortion—test them out. This will be the roof of the house, so glue it to the top.

You can see that by taking a material that can be distorted in several directions and combining it with similar materials in different dimensions, you can make a remarkably strong structure. This is the reason your house is strong enough to withstand strong winds, why you can fill it with guests for a party, and why the weight of snow on the roof doesn't crush it.

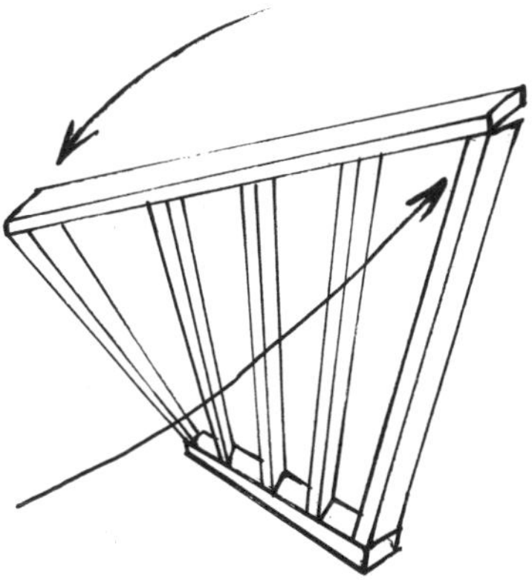

twisting

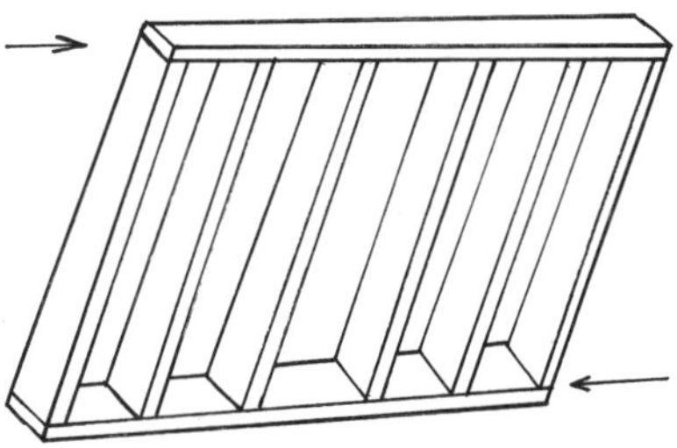

collapsing

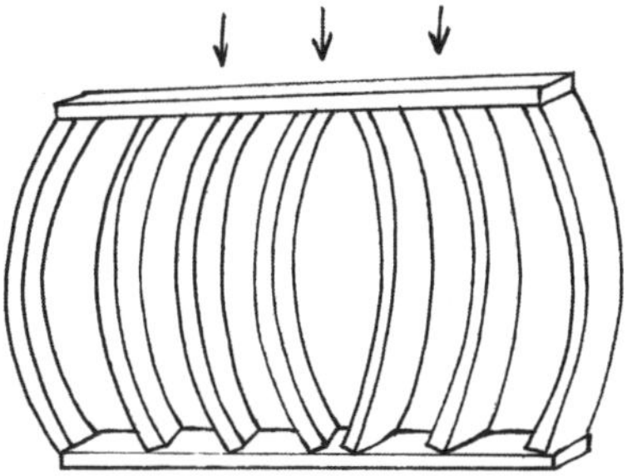

compressing

22-3 Testing for Distortion

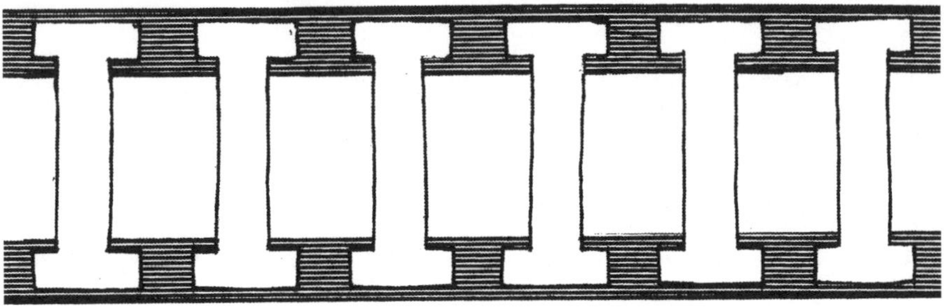

22-4 Cross Section of a Wall

Resource Connections

- Building a House by Ken Robbins
- Housebuilding For Children by Les Walker

TAKING IT FURTHER

1. Make a model of your own house, adhering as closely as possible to the frame construction principles.
2. Visit a construction site and view actual wood frames being put together.
3. Visit a building site of an office building and compare structural differences. Look for I-beams and frames.
4. Look for triangles and I-beams in machinery in your home and community. They are not always obvious, so some detective work might be necessary.

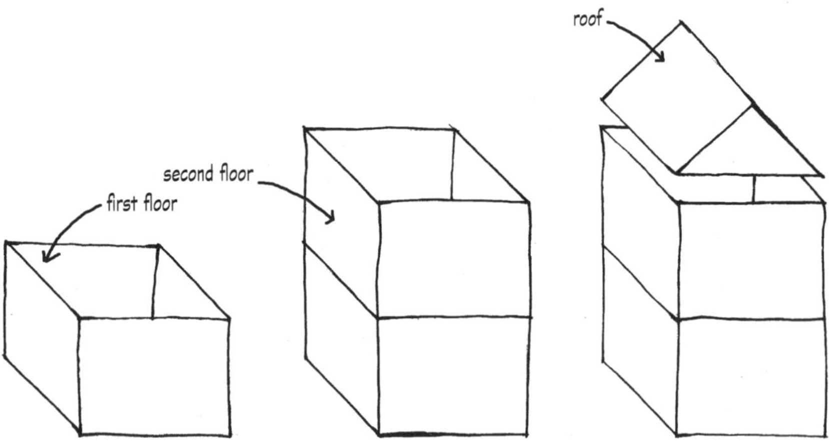

22-5 Model House

Flower Pigments

What's It All About?

What is colour? A plant's colour is produced by pigments (chemical compounds that absorb specific colours of light). The light from the sun is made up of all colours (red, orange, yellow, blue, green and purple) and when viewed all together they create the appearance of whiteness.

A pigment absorbs one or more colours, allowing other colours to reflect back into our eyes. For example, red petals absorb blue, green, yellow, orange, and purple light but not the red that we see. White substances like paper do not absorb any of the colours of sunlight and hence reflect it all into our eyes as whiteness. Black substances absorb all the components of the sun's light—blackness is the absence of light, hence the absence of any colour. Black substances warm up rapidly in the sun because the energy of all the colours of light is absorbed and converted into heat energy.

In this activity, you will learn how to chemically separate the pigments in flowers and other plant parts, and experiment to find which portions of which plants have the most types of pigments.

Going Ahead

1. You will use two solvent mixes to separate pigments. One might work better than the other, depending on the flowers you choose.
   - Solvent 1: 1/2 cup of water, 1/2 cup of rubbing alcohol, plus a dash of white vinegar.
   - Solvent 2: A cup of white vinegar.
2. Start with several clean dry jars, and use half of them for solvent 1 and half for solvent 2. Pour about 1 cm of solvent into the each jar. Put their lids on.
3. Cut the coffee filters into strips. Make sure they are narrower, and about 5 mm shorter than the jar.

What You Will Need

- Clear glass jars
- Several coffee filters
- Rubbing alcohol
- Water
- White vinegar
- Sticky tape

4. Take a flower petal and crush it into a small spot on the filter strip about 2 cm from the edge. Use the handle of a spoon or fork. You should see some colour on the filter. Get as much colour as possible. Then remove any bits of petal, and let the spot dry. You can spot several different types of flower onto one filter.

5. Carefully lower the strip into the jar, letting the end dip into the solvent. Tape the top end across the middle of the jar's mouth (see 23-1 Filter Strip in the Jar). Don't let the strip touch the sides of the jar. Wait and watch.

6. The solvent will rise up the paper by capillary action and dissolve the pigments in the spot. Different pigments will move up the strip at different speeds, depending on their unseen chemical molecular structure. After a suitable time—sometimes it can take hours—there should be one to several spots on the paper corresponding to the different pigments. This procedure is called chromatography, and it's used extensively in science to separate the components of mixtures of chemicals.

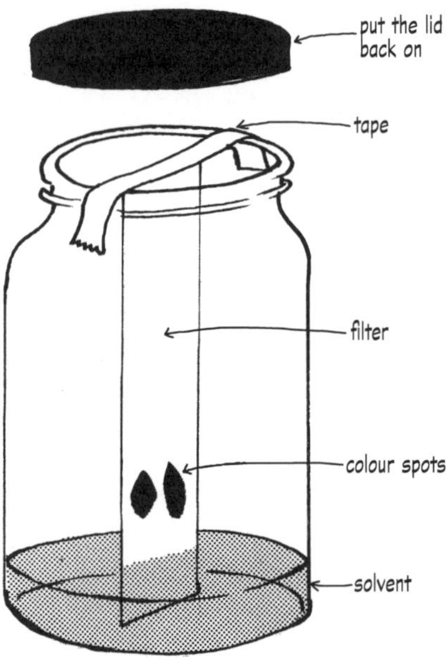

23-1 Filter Strip in the Jar

7. After separation, hang the paper up to dry.

8. For each run, record the solvent used, the flower type, the colour of the flower, the numbers of spots produced, the colours of the spots, the distance the spots moved, and the distance the solvent moved.

9. Calculate the relative mobility for each spot:

- the distance the spot moved divided by the distance the solvent front moved.

This number is constant for any type of pigment in a specific solvent, and can be used when comparing pigments.

10. If the experiment doesn't work the first time, try again. Then try to answer the following questions:
- Which colours of flowers in your garden or neighbourhood contain the most pigments, or produce the greatest number of spots? Consider flowers that are red, orange, yellow, blue, green and purple (or as many as are available).
- Does any flower have only one pigment (spot)?
- Which pigment moves the fastest? The slowest? (Be sure to specify the solvent because you cannot compare speeds observed using different solvents.)
- Was one solvent particularly good at separating the pigments of one plant?
- Was one solvent particularly good at separating certain colours of pigments?

Taking It Further

1. Try the same technique on leaves, especially in the fall when colours change. Then try it on lichens (see Activity 8—Getting to Like Lichens).
2. Try the same technique on brightly coloured fruits such as strawberries, raspberries and salmonberries (even the canned ones are worth an attempt).
3. Do a systematic study on roses of different types. Many roses are hybrids (formed by breeding two different roses together). Can you detect any hybrids by the pigment content? (If a rose with pigment A is bred with a rose with pigment B then the hybrid should have both A and B.)

Resource Connections

- *My Science Book of Colour* by Neil Ardley
- *Colour, from Rainbows to Lasers* by Franklyn M. Branley

What's It All About?

Streams and ponds contain many interesting animals that you rarely see. As part of the biodiversity of our natural ecosystems, these small—and mostly unappreciated—creatures are nevertheless important.

In this activity, you will go on a fishing expedition in freshwater streams and ponds, looking for animals without backbones, and using meat as bait. Two types of animals you should expect to see are flatworms—about 1 cm long with arrow-shaped heads—and leeches—larger segmented worms, related to earthworms, but characterized by a blood-sucking parasitic lifestyle (see 24-1 Freshwater Critters). These creatures have an undeserved bad reputation. Introducing yourself to them as subjects of interest and beauty can change these perceptions and remind you that even such inconspicuous life forms have a right to live.

This activity might not work well at some sites and might require a few attempts at different spots.

What You Will Need

- A notebook and pencil
- Pieces of liver or other inexpensive meats (about 10 cm x 5 cm)
- A string
- Glass jars with lids (baby food jars will do)
- A flat-bottomed glass baking dish
- A soft paint brush

Going Ahead

1. Take a trip to a local stream or pond. Tie a piece of liver onto the end of a string. Holding onto the other end, throw the string into the water, letting the liver rest on the bottom. Tie your end to a tree or a stick. Leave the liver in the water for at least an hour (you could even leave it overnight) to allow the critters to find the bait. Do the same thing in a different stream or pond.
2. Pull the liver out slowly and carefully, and place it in the glass dish. Examine it carefully for animals that might be eating it and are still attached. If you see interesting animals, use a wet paint brush to gently pry them off the liver and

onto the bottom of the dish.

3. Either take the animals home for study, or study them on the spot. If you do take them home, collect an extra jar of water from the stream. (Most animals prefer water from their home stream to tap water).

4. Make drawings of the animals, and note their size, colour, body structures, movements, collection site and date.

5. Try feeding them and observe the way they react to the meat (liver, steak, dog food, cat food and so on). Remove the water muddied by food and replace it with some of the fresh water you brought from the original collection site.

6. Study how the animals respond to light and dark conditions. Try covering half the dish with aluminum foil.

7. You can keep the animals at home for a little while as long as you make sure they are cool—try placing them outside in a shady spot or in the refrigerator. Be sure to return them to their original location before two days are up.

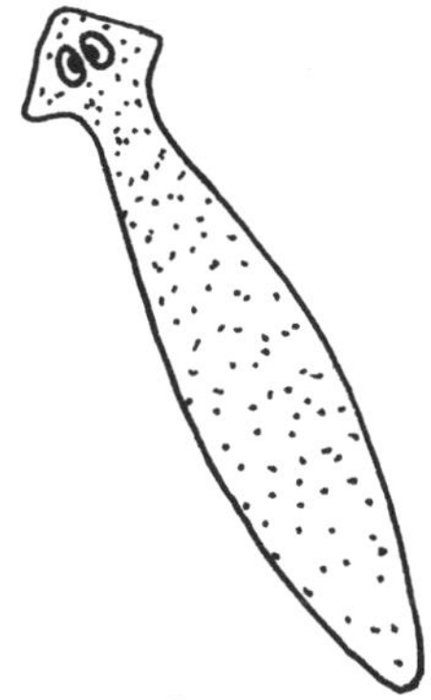

flatworm

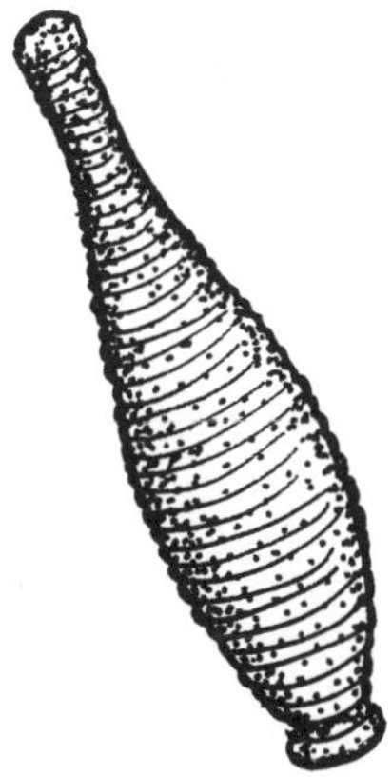

leech

24-1 Freshwater Critters

Taking It Further

1. Leeches are parasites. Read about parasites and their life cycles—think about how these animals have adapted for survival. What types of structures have they evolved into to allow them to follow their particular lifestyle?

2. Can you think of some plants that are parasites? Are there any in your community? (See Activity 12 - Mushroom Spore Prints for one idea.)

3. Not all animals that connect themselves to other animals are parasites. Look for other types of relationships in your neighbourhood. How would you classify cowbirds? Cuckoos? Lichens? 'Cleaner fish' that live in the gills of other fish?

Resource Connections

- Freshwater Plenarians of North America by Ranan Kenk
- Leeches by Lynn M. Stone

25 Rock Identification

What's It All About?

In some respects, rocks are like cookies. All cookies are made from just a few basic ingredients: flour, sugar, butter, and water. Some include chocolate chips, whereas others include nuts, but the essential ingredients are present in all cookies. The differences are the result of the manner and proportions in which these ingredients are combined, and the way in which they are baked. The same is true for rocks. Almost all rocks are made up of just a few elements. These few elements are combined in a much larger variety of ways to make minerals. Minerals, in turn, are mixed together to make the variety of rocks we find around us.

Black, white, and pink speckled rocks, rounded white rocks, purple rocks, shiny brown or black rocks, and holey black rocks—these are typical of the rocks that can be found along rivers or streams or lakes or ocean beaches.

How can we identify them?

Often when scientists want to identify things that have many similar characteristics, they use a key. A key is simply a set of logical steps you need to go through to decide between many alternative possibilities. The key that you will use in this activity can help you to identify many common rocks. You should realize, however, that small samples of some rocks can be very difficult to positively identify, so this key just provides a starting point and a way to narrow down the possibilities.

This activity is a good introduction to scientific observation and classification methods, and to geology.

What You Will Need

- A nail or knife
- A magnifying lens
- Possibly a hammer and safety glasses

Going Ahead

1. Use the rock key below at a rocky beach, or try

using it on sample rocks that you have already collected. Start at number 1 on the key. There you will find two choices: 1(a) and 1(b). Decide which choice best describes your rock and follow the directions that choice gives you to the next number in the key. For example, if choice 1(b) best matches your rock, you skip numbers 2 to 8 and go on to number 9 where you again make a choice regarding your rock. Continue through the key in this manner until you reach the point where the key gives a name to your rock. Be sure to read all of the choices at each number carefully before making a choice. Remember that you want to make the best choice and sometimes you will have to use careful observation and judgment to do so.

It helps to have a clean rock surface to look at. Wear safety glasses when using a hammer. Crack off a chip of rock, or break it in half to expose clean surfaces.

The Rock Key:

1.(a) Contains grains that are bigger than grains of sand. Go to 2.

1.(b) Formed from grains that are equal to or smaller than grains of sand. Go to 9.

2.(a) Composed of interlocking grains and includes individual minerals that are easy to recognize. Go to 3.

2.(b) Grains that appear glued together and not interlocking. Go to 8.

3.(a) Composed mainly of minerals that are mostly of one type. Go to 4.

3.(b) Contains large interlocking grains (about 1 to 2 mm in length) and different types of individual minerals that are easy to recognize. Go to 5.

4.(a) Composed mainly of shiny minerals (mica) in small sheets, like pages in a book. Small red minerals (garnets) may be embedded in the sheets. **Mica Schist**

4.(b) Composed mainly of large, usually whitish crystals. **Marble**

5.(a) Appears banded with light coloured and dark coloured regions. **Gneiss** (pronounced "nice")

5.(b) Contains large interlocking grains but not banded. Go to 6.

6.(a) Almost all the grains are large in size (typically 1 to 2 mm in length, or more). Go to 7.

6.(b) Large grains (which may be light or dark coloured) embedded in a small grained mass. **Porphyry**

7.(a) Overall appearance of the rock is dark. **Gabbro**

7.(b) Mostly made of grains of dark minerals but with some (about one quarter to one third) white minerals. **Diorite**

7.(c) Made of a mix of dark coloured grains, white grains, and often some pink grains. **Granite**

8.(a) Made up of large rounded rocks and small pieces glued together. **Conglomerate**

8.(b) Made up of broken, large fragments of rock and small pieces glued together. **Breccia**

9.(a) Grains smaller than sand. Go to 10.

9.(b) Grains the size of sand that appear to be glued together. Often grains will break from these rocks when they are scraped with a nail and they may appear layered. **Sandstone**

10.(a) Rock with distinct layers. Go to 11.

10.(b) Rock without distinct layers. Go to 12.

11.(a) Hard and brittle, layered rock with a greyish black and somewhat shiny appearance and parallel or nearly parallel flat surfaces. **Slate**

11.(b) Formed from very fine grains (about the size of flour) glued together in layers. Colours range from light brown to dark gray. **Shale**

12.(a) Very fine grained rock. Grains are so fine that it is difficult to see individual grains. Go to 13.

12.(b) Fine grained but individual grains are apparent when the rock is observed without a magnifying lens. Go to 15.

13.(a) Whitish, hard rock. **Quartzite**

13.(b) All other colours. Go to 14.

14.(a) Greenish coloured rocks. These may be one of a range of metamorphic rocks. If quite soft and with a soapy feel, then **Serpentine**. Harder green rocks may be **Chlorite** or **Jade**.

14.(b) A hard, red coloured rock, generally not much bigger than a golf ball in size. **Jasper**

14.(c) Black rock that looks like glass. **Obsidian**

15.(a) Grains that are interlocking because they were formed from a molten mass. Small crystals are evident. Though these rocks will break, they are usually hard and it is really difficult to break grains from them with a nail. They may contain holes and look like a sponge. Go to 16.

15.(b) Rocks that can be very similar in appearance to those described in 14(a) except that they are often (though not always) not as hard so that grains can be broken from them with a nail with moderate difficulty and they can be scratched with a nail. Colour may range from gray to nearly white. **Limestone**

16.(a) Black rock, often with holes. **Basalt**

16.(b) Dark gray, fine grained rock. **Andesite**

16.(c) Light gray, fine grained rock. **Rhyolite**

Taking It Further

1. Collect a few common rocks from several places in the community and try using the rock key to identify them. Then look up the rocks in a rock identification book and see if your rock

resembles the picture in the book. You may have a rock identification book in your home already that you could use, or you may be able to borrow one from your local library. Practice identifying rocks with the rock key and then confirming your identification with the book until you are confident in your ability to use the rock key successfully.

2. Make a collection of rocks of different types. Display them on shelves, labeled with name and collection site.

3. Visit rock shops to examine more varieties of rocks.

4. Check out the rocks when you go on vacation; bring home some interesting examples not found in your community.

5. Join a rock club.

6. Try identifying the kinds of rocks used in buildings and rock walls that you find near your home. What kinds of rocks are used for these purposes? What are the characteristics that make them especially good for use in buildings or walls?

7. What are the common types of rocks that occur naturally in the area near your home? Can you relate these rock types to the geographical features that you see around you?

Resource Connections

- A Look at Rocks: From Coal to Kimberlite by Jo S. Kittinger
- Spotter's Guide to Rocks and Minerals by Alan R. Wooley

Meet a Scientist

Catherine Hickson studies volcanoes

What do you do?

I study volcanoes. There are hundreds of volcanoes in the Pacific Northwest. Mount Baker is expected to erupt within the next century, but the eruption will most likely be small. There are many volcanoes in northern BC, including small cindercones that may erupt even sooner than Mount Baker. These eruptions are not dangerous, but incredibly interesting!

What made you want to study volcanoes?

I've been interested in the world around me for as long as I can remember. My father was a teacher, and loved to hunt, fish, and hike in the outdoors.

My mother loved outdoorsy things too, and both my parents encouraged me to ask questions about the natural world. I had a rock collection, and I remember lots of summer trips to national and provincial parks. When I was a preschooler, I was fascinated by the hot springs in Yellowstone National Park. Now, as British Columbia's leading expert on volcanoes, I know that some of those hot springs are the result of the cooling magma from a volcanic explosion tens of thousands of years ago! I have been back to Yellowstone several times since my childhood to study the effects of that ancient volcano, and have traveled to study many other volcanoes as well.

I didn't always think I would be a scientist when I grew up. While I was in high school, I was on the swim team. It didn't really seem like my interest in mountains and valleys was something to build a career on, so I decided to follow my love of swimming by studying recreation in university. It wasn't until after a break in my university days that I took a geology course. I enjoyed it so much that I thought maybe this is something I could do for a living! After I got a degree in geology, I went on to study four more years to get a Ph.D. in volcanology, the science of volcanoes.

Tell us a story about an exciting time or event in your career.

I was camping near Mount St Helens, Washington, on May 18, 1980, when it had the largest volcanic eruption in the conterminous United States this century! My husband and I were lucky to get out alive, but I'm pleased to report that scientists have learned a great deal from that explosion. We are now much better able to predict when a volcano might erupt and how big the eruption will be, so we can give people days or even weeks of warning.

What advice do I have for children who wonder what they will be when they grow up? Follow your passion! If science is really what tickles your interest, pursue it! If you're doing something you're excited about, whatever it is, you will do well.

Simple Machines

What's It All About?

People carry simple machines with them all the time; they make use of them every day. Many of the implements you use in and around your home are simple machines. Your arms and teeth are simple machines, and so are tools like knives, pliers, shovels, and hammers. Sports equipment like hockey sticks, tennis racquets, and baseball bats are also simple machines.

Every time you use a simple machine, you apply a force to the machine and the machine applies the force to some object. When it is applied to the object, however, the effect of the force is changed. The force can change direction, amount, and/or speed.

These are the main types of simple machines

What You Will Need

- A notebook and pencil
- Junk for building inventions (blocks of wood, elastics, wheels, tubing, plasticene, marbles, etc.)

Levers:

At its most basic, a lever consists of three parts: the lever itself (some sort of bar or arm); the fulcrum (a point on which it turns); and, the object to be moved, like a rock (see 26-1 Lever). It would be very difficult to lift the rock with your own strength but with the help of the lever, it is much easier.

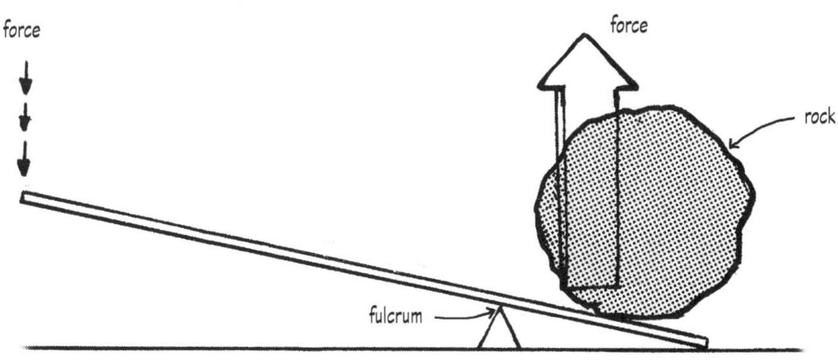

26-1 Lever

A pair of pliers is another example of a lever. When you use pliers, you squeeze the handles and the force is applied between the jaws. The inwards force applied on the handles causes an inwards force in the opposite direction at the jaw. And the force at the jaw is greater than that at handle because the distance from the handle to the fulcrum is greater than that from the jaw to the fulcrum. In this example, you don't want to increase the speed of the jaws, rather, you want to be able to exert a greater force than would be possible without the use of the pliers.

Inclined planes

Like levers, inclined planes come in a number of shapes. On an inclined plane, you must travel a greater distance, but it is easier to move up the incline than to climb straight up. For example, it makes your work easier to push a rock up a ramp than to lift it straight up (see 26-2 Inclined Plane). The stairs you climb in a building can also be considered to be an inclined plane. Cutting edges also use inclined planes:

26-2 Inclined Plane

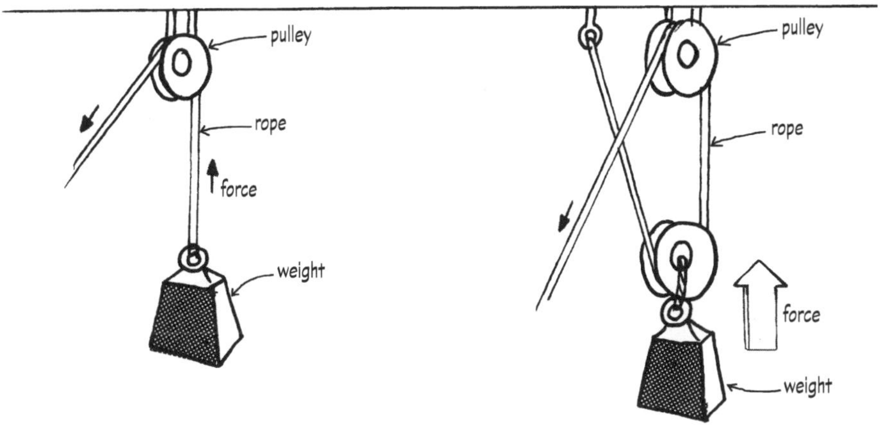

26-3 Rope and Pulley

two inclined planes back to back to make a wedge. Screw threads are also inclined planes. In this case the inclined plane is wrapped around in a spiral.

Wheels

Wheels are everywhere. Along with axles, they are simple machines that can be used to move a load. A disc is designed to turn around an axle which passes through the disc's centre. The axle may be fixed to the wheel so it can turn when the axle rotates, or the wheel may spin freely on the axle. Wheels make work easier by reducing friction: imagine what carrying things would be like if we had no wheels!

A rope and pulley is a member of the wheel family and a simple machine as well. You don't see these as commonly as levers and inclined planes, but nevertheless they are very important. Some types of window blinds use ropes and pulleys to control them. If you look at a crane in a construction site you may see other examples.

A rope and single pulley simply changes the

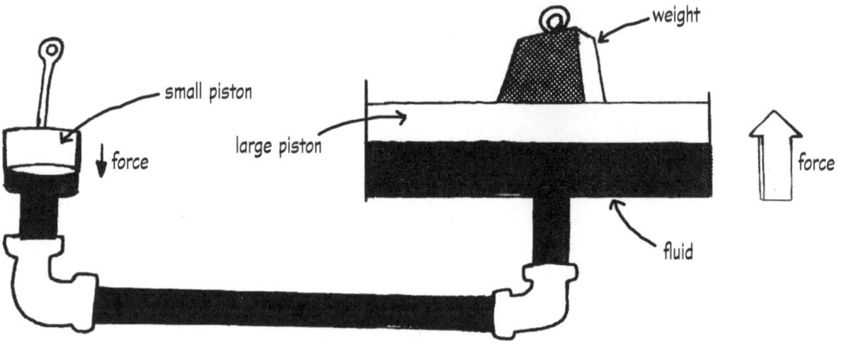

26-4 Hydraulic System

direction of force. Two pulleys increase the amount of force applied to an object being lifted, making work even easier (26-3 Rope and Pulley).

Hydraulics

In many cases hydraulic systems have taken the place of ropes and pulleys in modern machinery. These hydraulic systems are the fourth type of simple machine. Hydraulic machines machines work by confining fluids (liquids and gases) in enclosed spaces. Examples are the hydraulic brake system on cars or the hydraulic cylinders on bulldozers and excavators. Big tractor-trailer trucks use hydraulic brake systems that use air as the fluid (otherwise each time a trailer was connected or disconnected liquid could be lost from the system).

When the piston is pushed down on one cylinder, it pushes on the fluid in the cylinder. The fluid transfers this force all the way through the connecting pipe to the second cylinder where it puts force on the second piston. Since this piston has a bigger surface area on which the fluid pushes, however, the force on this large piston is greater than that on the small one (see 26-4 Hydraulic System).

Imagine using a bicycle pump to pump up a flat tire on a car. In this example the bicycle pump contains the small piston and the tire itself is the large piston. As you pump air into the tire you would raise the corner of the car.

This example of a hydraulic machine shows another feature that is common to all simple machines. They all make work easier because they change direction of force, the size of force, or the speed of an object, but they do not make less work! Without the simple hydraulic machine of the bicycle pump and tire you probably could not lift the corner of the car. With it you can lift that corner but you would be hot and tired from raising the corner and from all the work you did against friction and from moving parts of the simple machine.

Springs and elastics

Springs and elastics do at least two important things: they help return things to their original place like a door spring does, and they also store energy. When a spring or elastic is released it releases energy. This is how wind-up toys and watches work.

Going Ahead

1. Look around your home for examples of simple machines.
2. Decide if your example is a lever, an inclined plane, a wheel, a pulley, a spring or a hydraulic system. Is it a combination of different types of simple machines?
3. Figure out what it is that the simple machine does—does it increase or change the direction of

the force? Does it increase the speed? How does the machine accomplish this change?

4. Complete a table like the one below:

Device	Type of machine	Increases or decreases force	Changes direction of force	Changes speed of force	How does it work?

5. In each case draw a sketch of the device, or the part of the device you are working on, and show clearly the simple machine principle behind it.

6. Analyze these devices:
   - corkscrew
   - door lock
   - all the parts of a Swiss army knife
   - fishing reel
   - claw of a hammer
   - toilet flushing mechanism
   - bicycle pedal
   - stairs
   - window latch
   - lifting door hinge
   - hockey stick
   - water pistol
   - lawnmower

Taking It Further

1. Invent these machines, using materials found around your house or apartment:
   - a machine that will strike a match and light it;
   - a machine that will allow you to turn off your bedroom ceiling light without having to get out of bed;
   - a drum that beats when the wind blows;
   - a machine that can turn a chocolate chip cookie over onto its back without breaking it;
2. In each machine you make, identify the levers, inclined planes, wheels and springs.
3. Look for examples of simple machines around your community. Good places to start looking are construction sites, industrial plants and automotive garages—places where heavy things are moved. For additional examples, think of places where things need to go faster and further; sports activities are a good place to start.

Resource Connections

- *Gateway Simple Machines Series (Wheels, Pulleys, Inclined Planes, Levers)* by Christopher Lampton
- *Simple Machines* by Fran Whittle
- http://www.fi.edu.qu97/spotlight3/spotlight3.html
- http://seamonkey.ed.asu.edu/~hixson/index/machines.html

27 Meet Spaceship Earth

What's It All About?

The term 'Spaceship Earth' emphasizes the fact that our planet is a self-contained system hurtling through space. As people traveling on a 'spaceship', we have to be careful with the management of our resources and the disposal of our waste products.

In this activity, you will make a reasonable measurement of the size of the planet, and calculate our relative distance from the sun and moon. These measurements are based on the work of ancient Greek astronomers. They will help you visualize our planet as a ball moving through space, and give you a sense of our relative position in the solar system.

What You Will Need

- A notebook and pencil
- A piece of white paper
- A stick about 20 cm long
- A wooden block
- A protractor
- A global sundial (see Activity 20 - A Global Sundial)

Going Ahead

Estimating the size of the planet Earth.

1. Twenty-two hundred years ago, Greek astronomer Eratosthenes first calculated the size of the planet. He noticed that at midday, the sun shone straight down a well because it was positioned directly overhead. Yet he knew that at that very moment, in a different city, the sun cast a shadow at an angle. Eratosthenes was able to calculate the circumference of the Earth, using the distance between the two cities and the angle at which the sun cast a shadow in the second city (27-1 Eratosthenes' Method for Calculating the Circumference of the Earth).

Using your town as one point and a town directly to the south as another, you too can calculate the circumference of the Earth using the same method as Eratosthenes.

Set up a stick vertically on a flat surface outside. Your stick shouldn't be longer than 20 cm. At midday, measure the length of the Sun's shadow.

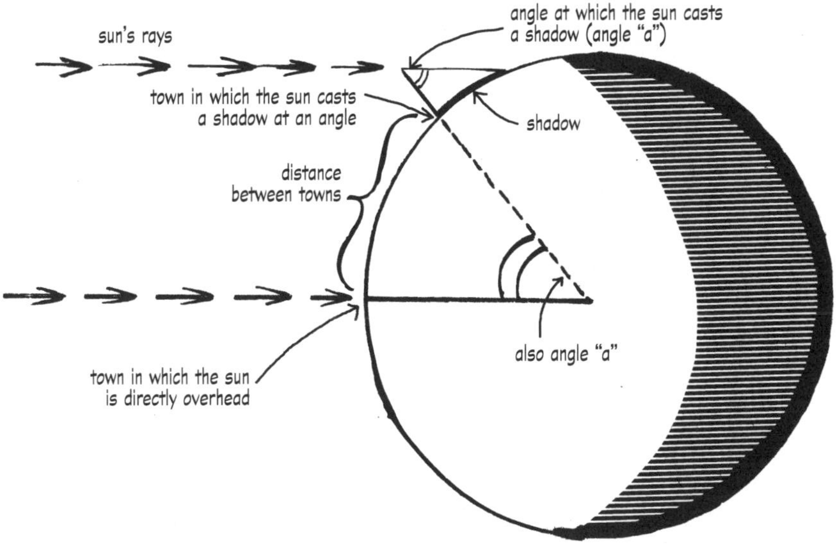

27-1 Eratosthenes' Method for Calculating the Circumference of the Earth

(Remember that at noon the shadow will be shorter than at any other time of day.) Then draw a triangle the same size as the one made by the stick and its shadow, making sure the angle between them is 90 degrees. Measure the angle between the height of the stick and the line connecting it to its shadow (see 27-2 Calculating the Circumference of the Earth).

2. Take the global sundial (see Activity 20-A Global Sundial) and use your sun stand to find the town directly to the south—on the same line of longitude—where the sun is directly overhead. This town will be the equivalent of Eratosthenes' town where the sun shone down the well. On the globe or map, mea-

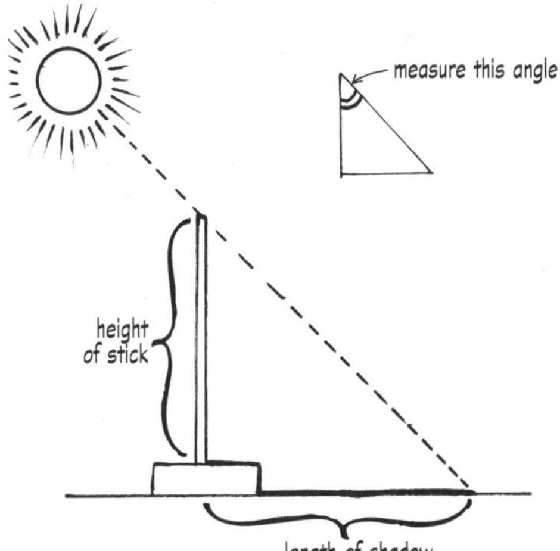

27-2 Calculating the Circumference of the Earth

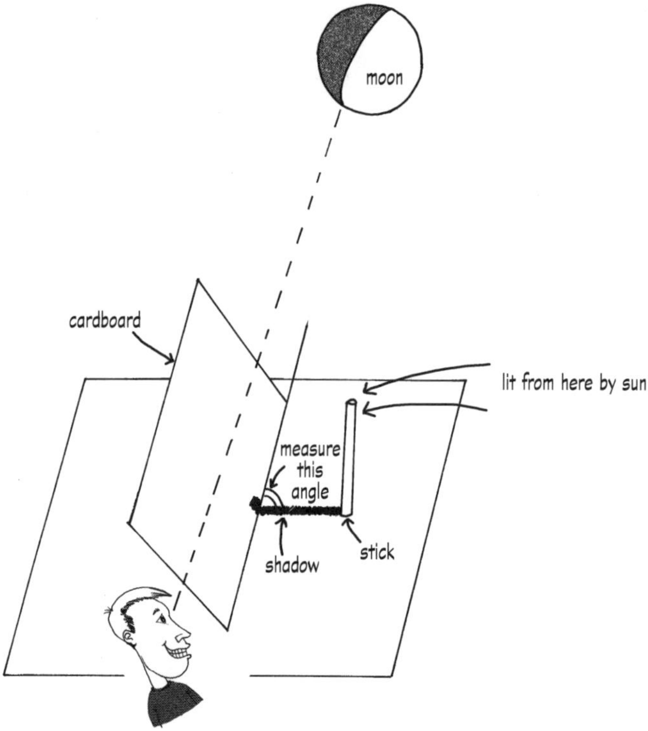

27-3 Measuring the Angle Between the Sun, the Earth and the Moon

sure the distance between that town and your own.

3. To calculate the circumference of the Earth use this method:

- (360 divided by your angle) x distance from southern town = circumference of Earth

Once you have the circumference, you can calculate the radius of the Earth because

- circumference = 2 x π x radius (π—pronounced 'pie'—is a mathematical constant, approximately equal to 22/7, which is about 3.14.) Hence, circumference = 6.28 x radius

So,

- radius = circumference divided by 6.28

These simple measurements give us the basic

dimensions of our planet. Check your measurement against the 'official' measurement and see how accurate it is.

Estimating the relative distance to the Moon and the Sun.

1. Twenty three hundred years ago, another Greek astronomer, Aristarchus, figured out a way to measure the relative distances to the Moon and the Sun. You are about to use his method.

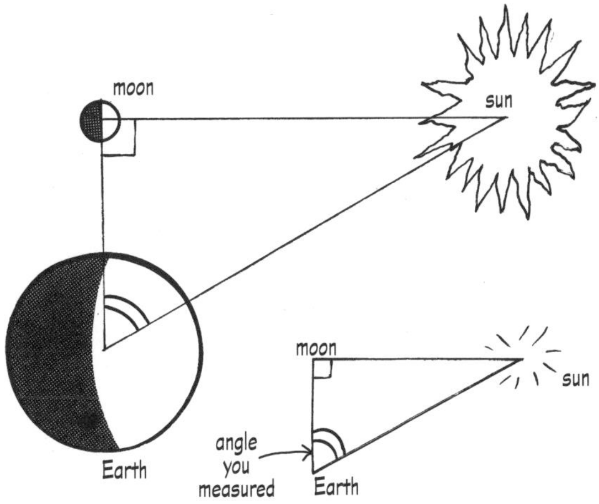

27-4 Triangle Between the Sun, the Earth and the Moon

2. Find out on what day the Moon will be half full **before sunset**. The newspaper, or the library, is a good place to get this information.

3. Hold a piece of cardboard vertically on a flat surface and sight a line to the Moon. Set up a stick so it casts a shadow that reaches to the cardboard (see 27-3). Measure the angle between the shadow and the bottom of the cardboard. Because your stick is lit by the Sun, the angle you measured is the angle between the Sun, the Earth and the Moon.

Because exactly half the Moon is visible, the angle from the Earth to the Moon to the Sun must be 90 degrees. Recreate the triangle in 27-4 Triangle Between You, the Moon, and the Sun on a piece of paper. The relative proportions of this triangle will be the same no matter what size it is so by measuring the two sides representing the distances to Moon and Sun, you can calculate their relative distances from Earth.

- How many more times distant is the Sun than the Moon?

TAKING IT FURTHER

1. Extend your study to the movement of the moon. Record the movements and degree of fullness of the moon as often as possible.
    - does it always move in the same direction?
    - does it always rise in the same place on the horizon?
    - does it always rise at the same time?
    - when it rises, is it always in the same degree of fullness?
2. Make a simple model, using balls, fruit, and a flashlight to show how your observed patterns of Moon movement and shadow are produced. Pay particular attention to the positions of the Moon's appearance and disappearance each night. If the Moon were on an equatorial orbit around the Earth, would these positions differ each night?
3. The Earth spins faster than the Moon orbits (how does this affect your above deductions)? If the Moon appears to be moving from East to West, does that prove that the Moon is moving in this direction?

Resource Connections

- The Librarian Who Measured Earth by Kathryn Lasky
- Exploring Earth in Space by Robert Stephenson and Roger Browne

An Endangered Habitat

This activity can only be done in the coastal region of BC, between Victoria and Nanaimo, and in the Gulf Islands.

What's It All About?

The dry coastal Douglas fir zone is one of BC's most threatened ecological zones. It extends from the southern tip of Vancouver Island up the east coast to Nanaimo and includes all of the Gulf Islands. The climate is Mediterranean-like, drier and warmer than the surrounding areas, largely because the region is in a rain shadow. The most conspicuous and different part of the dry coastal Douglas fir zone is the southern slopes on the edge of the ocean or lakes. It's a joyous open parkland with grassy meadows, spectacular spring wildflowers, and trees found nowhere else in BC or Canada. Unfortunately, this terrain has become a magnet for housing development and most of the parkland has disappeared. Only pockets remain and they're mostly threatened.

In this activity, you will learn to distinguish different ecological life zones after finding key indicator plants. This will heighten your awareness of ecological differences across the province, focusing on the problems of threatened habitats which are just as important as threatened species.

What You Will Need

- A notebook and pencil
- A plant book
- Possibly a camera (you will probably want to take photographs)

Going Ahead

1. When in the Victoria/Nanaimo/Gulf Island area, plan a trip to find this zone. The early springtime (April, May) is particularly rewarding, as this is the time the annual wildflower bloom occurs. Parks are the best bet, for example in Victoria, Thetis Lake Park, Mount Douglas Park and Mill Hill Park are all excellent. There are several parks around Nanaimo as well. On Galiano Island, Bluffs Park

and Bellhouse Park are also easily accessible. Canoeing or kayaking is an excellent way to find the dry coastal Douglas fir zone. If you are hunting for the dry parkland part of this zone, look for the most conspicuous indicator trees: Arbutus, with its unusual smooth coppery-orange bark; and Garry Oak, the only BC-native oak (see 28-1 Trees of the Dry Coastal Douglas Fir Zone).

2. Look for some typical plants that occupy this zone. Some of them are:

- Arbutus trees.
  - → coppery bark resembling human skin, often peeled back to reveal green inner bark.
  - → Canada's only broadleaf evergreen.
  - → Dark green rhododendron-like leaves.
  - → White heather-like flowers in May.
  - → Berries red to green.
- Garry oak.
  - → Typical oak leaves and bark.
  - → Trunks often highly twisted, and tumbling down rockfaces or banks.
  - → In the natural ecosystem the seedlings were probably established by fires.
- Spring gold.
  - → Flat clusters of small yellow flowers in an umbrella arrangement.
  - → Leaves like carrot leaves.
- Blue-eyed Mary.
  - → A short (5-10 cm) spring-blooming annual with small bright blue 'snapdragon'-like flowers inhabiting open meadows and bluffs.
- Sea blush.
  - → A spring-blooming annual with pink flower heads looking and smelling a bit like clover.
  - → Almost always found with Blue-eyed Mary.
  - → Both often found as spectacular carpets of blooms.

Arbutus

Garry Oak

28-1 Trees of the Dry Coastal Douglas Fir Zone

- Gold stars.
  - → Short very early-blooming annual, often in February.
  - → Yellow flowers like miniature sunflowers 5-10 cm high.
- Blue camas.
  - → Tall spring-blooming spikes of gorgeous blue flowers.
  - → Grow from subterranean bulbs, highly prized as food by First Nations.
- Chocolate lily.
  - → Unusual brown bell-like flower with checkerboard markings.
  - → Also grows from a bulb.

3. For each sighting of a particular plant type, note the name, date, location and the approximate number of plants. Make sketches of the plants—especially of their interesting features.

4. Make a quick map of the site, showing main features.

5. Assess the impact of various types of human activity on this habitat. What is the impact of visitors to the site who come to take in the natural beauty? Visitors, like you, have an impact that cannot be denied. Can you find evidence of the presence of visitors? Look for garbage, trampled plants, paths, or signs of vandalism. Look at the soil on and off the trails.

6. What is the impact of people who choose to make their home in this area? Is housing development minimal or widespread? Are there visible signs that this housing has had an impact on adjacent areas? Describe these. What might be the impact of shrinking the size of the coastal dry ecological zone?
7. Think about how we might maintain a balance between human activity and the natural environment. Come up with a proposal that would permit a balance to be struck between human activity and the continued survival of the dry Douglas fir zone. Write your proposal in the form of a letter to the editor of a local paper.

Taking It Further

1. Natural history societies often organize visits to these areas, especially in the spring when flowering is at its peak. These groups sometimes have access to sites on private property.
2. On the US side of the border, the same zone is found near Anacortes and on the San Juan Islands. These sites are also worth visiting.
3. Look for Blue-eyed Mary and Sea Blush seeds in specialty seed stores and grow your own native plant gardens.
4. Look for animals that might be adversely affecting the habitat by grazing on plants, for example, deer (introduced) and feral goats.

Resource Connections

- British Columbia: A Natural History by Richard Cannings and Sydney Cannings
- Wildflowers of the Pacific Northwest by Lewis J. Clark
- Trees, Shrubs and Flowers to Know in BC by C.P. Lyons and Bill Merrilees
- From Sidewalk to Seashore by Linda R. White and Janice Jellicoe

Meet A Scientist

Faizy Hudda is an environmental engineer

WHAT DO YOU DO?

I work on projects to investigate, test, and clean up sites with contaminated soil and groundwater. Soil and groundwater usually become polluted from human activities. Pollution can come from gas stations, dry cleaners, old heating oil tanks and lots of other activities that humans do. First, we investigate sites to look for risks of contamination, next we test the soil and groundwater by sampling it, and finally we clean it up by digging out the soil and pumping or treating the water, or we try to get rid of the pollution by other methods.

What made you want to be an environmental engineer?

I wanted to do something interesting and worthwhile and I wanted to work in a new, expanding field. Every day is different and challenging. Some days I work in the office talking to clients and writing reports; some days I am working in the field—outside—investigating, testing, and cleaning up contamination.

Tell us a story about an exciting time or event in your career.

Once I got to do a big audit for a forestry company. An audit is where we look at the past and current uses of a site and figure out how much it would cost to clean up the pollution. This project was very exciting to me since I had never done anything like it before and I knew I would be learning a lot. I learned about where pollutants and contaminants come from, how they get into soil, and the costs related to cleaning them up. I got to work all over Vancouver Island and the best part was flying around in helicopters all week. Up until that week I had never flown in a helicopter—it was great fun and a wonderful experience!

Alpine Meadows

What's It All About?

Some of the most spectacular sights in BC are its alpine meadows. Plants on high mountain sides are covered in snow for a large portion of the year, so they must complete their growth and reproductive cycles in the short summer period when the snow melts. Most flowering plants need to be fertilized to produce seeds (mountain plants accomplish this by rapidly blooming once the snow has melted). The bloom is simultaneous in many species, resulting in beautiful mixed carpets of flowers in the alpine meadows.

In this activity, you will learn about alpine plants; what they are, some of their names, the specialized conditions in which they live and their reproduction. You will also have an opportunity to enjoy this beautiful ecological zone that is unique, within Canada, to BC and Alberta.

Going Ahead

1. To do this activity at the peak of flowering, phone your local natural history society or local National or Provincial Parks officers, to find out how the alpine flowers are coming along. Most often this will be in July or August, depending on how quickly the snow melts.

2. Generally, the places with the easiest access are in Provincial or National Parks. Near Vancouver, Garibaldi Provincial Park is a good place to start, as there are three good access points—Black Tusk, Diamond Head and Singing Pass. The Whistler ski lift operates in summer and it provides rapid access to alpine areas. There are many access points in the Rockies. Manning Park is also a good spot. Local hiking books give useful tips on trails to the interesting areas. Be warned: you will be hiking, so wear a hat, bring water and lunch, and

What You Will Need

- A notebook and pencil
- Possibly a BC flower book
- Possibly a camera
- Binoculars

wear sun block and insect repellent.

3. When you arrive at a flowering meadow, observe the general lay of the land. Are there trees in the vicinity or are you close to, or beyond, the tree line? Does this tell you why the alpine plants are growing in full sunlight? If there are trees around, what do they look like? Are they the same size as their counterparts lower down on the mountain? What environmental conditions could explain their sizes and shapes? Look for samples of krummholtz— 'twisted wood'—low, gnarled trees.

4. Start cataloguing the flowering plants. Note the area, the date, whether the plants are in sun or shade, and make quick sketches of the most common types. Try to count the numbers of each type in one specific area, then move to another area that is a little different and repeat the counts.

5. Look for some of these common alpine meadow plants:

- Indian paintbrush. These have bright red or orange terminal leaves that look like petals.
- Lupines. These have blue or purple spikes of pea-like flowers.
- Anemones. They have white flowers that become 'tousle-headed' masses of hair-like fruits.
- Fleabanes. These have daisy-like flowers, with light purple petals and yellow centres.
- Arnicas. These plants have yellow daisy-like flowers.
- Louseworts. These plants show spikes of small yellowish-pink 'snapdragon' flowers, and have lacy, fern-like leaves.
- Penstemons. These have big blue or purple foxglove-like flowers, all pointing in one direction.

6. Alpine meadows are good places to study the habits of insect pollinators. Sit down quietly and follow one insect as it moves from flower to flower (see Activity 14-Animal Behaviour).
7. Write a short summary: "The botany of a BC alpine meadow at __________." Include which plants you found most interesting and why. Include a list of things you would like to find out about alpine plants.
8. Invent a conversation between a plant from the alpine environment and its counterpart at sea level. The plants could 'discuss' their experiences throughout the seasons and how life in each environment is special, how they have evolved to adapt to these conditions, etc.

Taking It Further

1. Once the alpine 'bug' has bitten, you will want to look at more meadows. Be sure to compare them in all the features you studied in the first one.
2. Alpine flowers are excellent subjects for photography. Make colour prints and include them in your notebook.

Resource Connections

- Mountain Flowers of British Columbia Provincial Parks by British Columbia Parks
- Alpine Wildflowers by J.E. Underhill

An Intertidal Voyage

What's It All About?

A trip to the beach can provide you with a multitude of experiences, and one of the most engaging is an investigation of the intertidal zone. This is the strip of beach between the low and high tide marks, an area in which the organisms are covered in sea water at high tide, but exposed to the air at low tide. The intertidal zone is home to a myriad of fascinating plants and animals, all uniquely adapted to living between the tides.

Each day, the incoming tide brings flooding, strong currents, varying water temperatures and aquatic predators. The receding tide reveals an ecosystem vulnerable to extreme heat and cold, drying winds and terrestrial predators.

While you explore the inhabitants of this complex and fragile community, you can also investigate plant and animal characteristics, predator-prey relationships, camouflage, animal behaviour and adaptations, habitats and biological classification. As you become acquainted with this exciting world, you will develop a sense of stewardship and assume the role of caretaker as well as visitor.

This activity turns a mere trip to the beach into an exploration of biodiversity, animal behaviour and marine ecology.

What You Will Need

- A notebook and pencil
- A small bucket
- Some zip lock bags
- Dip nets
- A field guide
- Magnifying lens

Going Ahead

1. It is important to think about beach etiquette before your trip. Think of ways to observe beach inhabitants without harming them. Rocks must be returned to their original spot and placed in their original position. Picking up a beach rock is similar to taking the roof off your own home. There are animals that live on the rock's underside as well as underneath it and if left exposed, they will quickly die from heat, desiccation (drying out) or

predation. Always watch where you step as someone may be living underfoot. If you pick up an animal, keep it safe in a bucket or baggie. Every organism must be returned to their home spot. Be careful when handling animals which protect themselves through jaws, spines, pincers and sharp outer shells.

2. Select a beach. A rocky beach will be more interesting than a sandy one because it provides more attachment sites for seaweeds and so will have more animals as well.

3. Choose a low tide day. Look at a tide table or the newspaper and think about how to interpret the tide charts. Look at a lunar calendar and think about how the phases of the moon affect the tides.

4. Once on the beach, mark the position of the tide line when you arrive with a stick or rock. During your visit, check your tide marker to see if the tide is receding or advancing. Try to identify the last high tide and low tide marks. These two marks define the intertidal zone (see 30-1 The Intertidal Zone).

5. You can begin your study by scouring the high-tide line for interesting beach objects. Look for discarded shells, shipworm riddled driftwood, marine algae (seaweeds) and the cast-off shells of crabs. Can you find an entire exoskeleton? Investigate the molt to determine where the crab exited its old shell.

6. Move to the mid-tide zone and investigate the inhabitants. On the surface of rocks, you will find small acorn barnacles and underneath the rocks, you will discover tiny periwinkles and small shore crabs.

7. The low-tide zone reveals larger shore crabs residing under the rocks along with worms, clams,

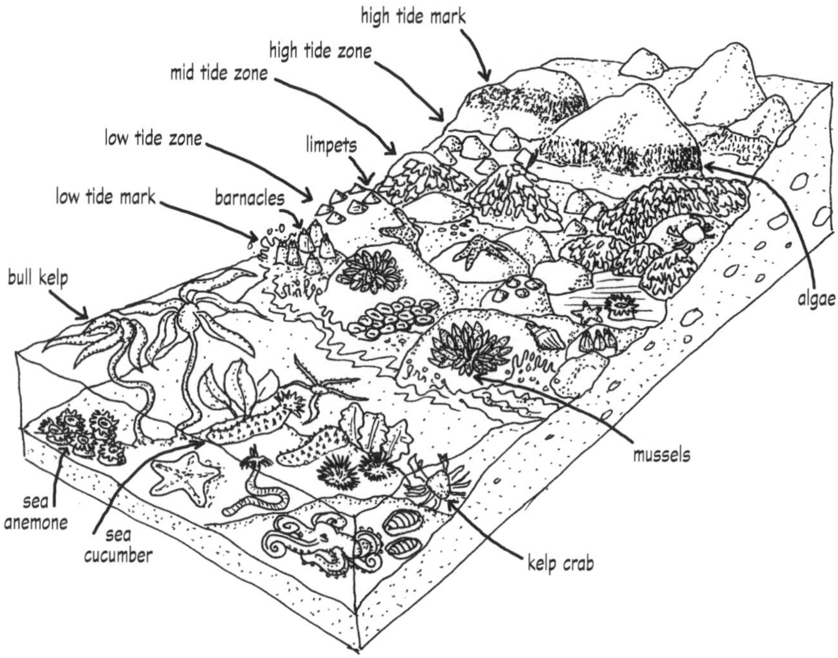

30-1 The Intertidal Zone

hermit crabs, sea anemones, starfish and fish such as blennies and clingfish. On the rock's undersurface, you may discover limpets, chitons, pill bugs and nudibranchs. Look for the nudibranch's jelly-like egg ribbons in the early spring. Attached to the rock's surface are blue mussels and the larger species of acorn barnacles. Look for rockweed isopods hidden among the camouflaging fronds of marine algae (seaweeds).

The intertidal area often has tide pools. In these pools, species are rarely exposed to the air, but they do experience extremes in water temperatures and predation from birds and terrestrial animals. Tidepool sculpins, crabs, limpets and whelks cruise the tidepools while barnacles, sea anemones and marine algae are permanent residents.

8. Use your notebook to record your beach obser-

vations. Include biological information, field notes, sketches, photos, and personal thoughts and experiences. Put your notebook in a zip lock bag to keep it dry.

Taking It Further

1. Observe a feeding barnacle. Find a group of submerged barnacles and watch as the crustacean's feathery appendages rake the water for a meal of plankton.
2. Find and compare a male and female crab. Male shorecrabs usually have larger pincers than females. Gently pick up some shore crabs and turn them over to compare abdomens. Male crabs have a pointed abdomen and the female's is rounded. In the spring, females carry a mass of tiny black eggs under the abdomen flap.
3. Observe the swimming technique of isopods. Gently place an isopod upside down in a tidepool and watch as it uses swimmeret plates to propel its body through the water. Female isopods carry their egg masses under these plates to protect them.
4. Observe how a crab moves and protects itself. When a shorecrab feels threatened, it will raise its pincers in a warning posture. Watch how it moves its appendages in a sideways motion as it scurries for cover.
5. Use a dip net to catch some tidepool residents such as blennies, sculpins, and shrimp. Take a closer look at them with your magnifying lens.
6. By looking at the high, middle and low regions of the intertidal zone, deduce the environments preferred by specific seaweeds. Is there any overlap of ranges?
7. Do a species inventory of one area. Select a reef, tidepool, rock or other intertidal area and

record the number and type of plant and animal species present.

8. Do a transect study. Lay a long length of string down the beach between the tide marks and record all the species you see from top to bottom.

9. Draw up a food web using your species inventory. Who are the predators and who are the prey?

10. Classify the organisms of the intertidal zone. You can start with crustaceans, fish, marine algae and mollusks. A successful classification is one that could be used by someone else to identify an individual intertidal organism.

11. Make a map depicting the different intertidal zones and their inhabitants.

12. Investigate human impact on the intertidal zone. Evaluate possible habitat destruction, garbage, pollution and over-harvesting.

13. Investigate how intertidal organisms protect themselves from changes in air and water temperature, desiccation, and predation during low tide, and wave shock, and predation during high tide.

14. Compare different types of beaches (rocky, sandy, cobblestone and mudflat, for example). Which species of intertidal life are unique to which areas? Also, compare intertidal zones on beaches with rough wave action to those in sheltered areas. Some organisms can be found in more than one area.

Resource Connections

- Beachwalker: Sea Life of the West Coast by Stefani Hewlett Paine
- Exploring the Seashore in BC, Washington and Oregon by Gloria Snively

Making a Cricket Thermometer

This activity can only be done in the interior of BC.

What's It All About?

In the Southern Interior of BC, the night air in summer is often full of the sounds of crickets. There are several species of crickets, but the Snowy Tree Crickets are a somewhat special species as they synchronize their chirping sound, producing a long series of monotonous—and loud—chanting. They make this sound by rubbing a rasp on one wing against a scraper on the other.

The frequency of chirps is temperature-dependent, so when it's warm, the crickets chirp more times per minute than when it's cold. In this activity, you will monitor the chirping frequency on different nights and then correlate it with air temperature. By doing this, you will develop a cricket thermometer that will tell you the temperature without the aid of a real thermometer.

Going Ahead

What You Will Need

- A notebook and pencil
- A wristwatch or clock that measures seconds
- A thermometer
- A flashlight

1. On a summer evening, go outside into the garden or park and listen to the night sounds. Try to identify the chirping sounds of crickets and in particular, the synchronized chanting of the Snowy Tree Cricket.
2. Measure the air temperature as accurately as possible using the thermometer. Count how many times the crickets chirp in one full minute and record this number. Do this count four or five times. Calculate the average number of chirps per minute for that time. If the air temperature seems to drop towards bedtime, make another series of observations.
3. On subsequent evenings, make more counts of chirping frequency and temperature.
4. When you have about ten readings, plot the

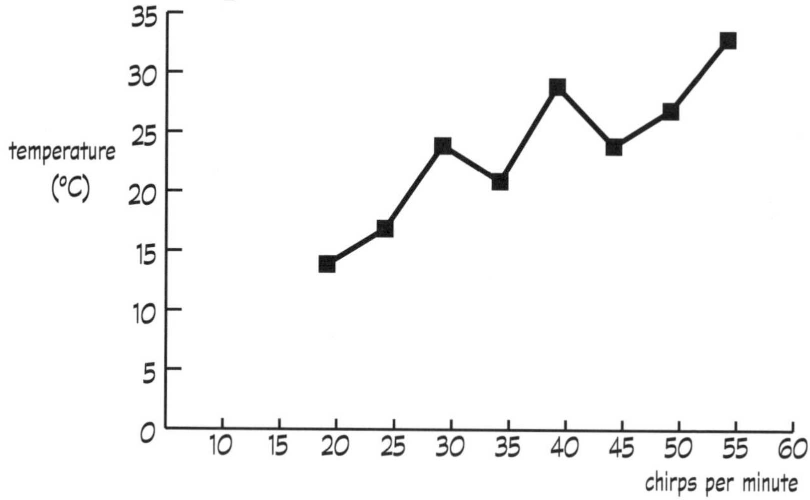

31-1 Chirping Frequency

average chirping frequency per minute against the air temperature (see 31-1). Join the dots. Do you see a roughly straight line? If you do, it means the chirping frequency is directly related to temperature. It is possible that you will not have a straight line, and in that case there is a more complex relationship between temperature and chirping.

5. Using a different coloured pen, draw a smooth line that represents the best fit through your dots. In other words, iron out all the kinks in your line joining the dots. This line of best fit represents your cricket thermometer. By knowing the cricket chirping frequency on any evening, you can immediately deduce the temperature.

Taking It Further

1. If your best fit is a straight line, can you deduce a formula to calculate the temperature?

For example, the formula might look like this (this one has been made up):

> "To find air temperature, simply take the number of chirps in a minute, multiply by three and add four."

2. Listen carefully to the noises of the night. Try to identify the possible source of each noise. Are they coming from:

   a. humans?

   b. animals?

   c. plants?

   d. non-living things?

3. Which of these sounds would you have heard standing on the same spot 200 years ago? Would there have been any sounds then that you do not hear today?

4. Classify the sounds you hear as having to do with:

   a. communication

   b. hunting

   c. alarm

   d. biologically meaningless

5. Look for night animals—bats, owls, insects and ground-dwelling mammals. With an adult, go for a night walk looking for animals that are active at night.

Resource Connections

- Wildlife at Night by Theodore S. Pettit
- Midnight Animals by Christopher Tunney

32 When Do Herons Give Up?

What's It All About?

Great blue herons are a familiar sight on the coast and lakes of BC. In this activity, you will observe the feeding behaviour of these majestic birds. They hunt for fish in the shallows, waiting patiently until they see a fish, and strike with their beaks. Herons have to judge whether they'll be able to catch anything in a given lake on any given day. If they can't make a catch relatively quickly, they must then find another place where the fishing is better.

The goal of this activity is to record the feeding behaviour of herons on different days and perhaps in different places and to deduce the relationship between the time it takes to catch a fish and the time it takes to give up.

What You Will Need

- A notebook and pencil
- A wristwatch with a second hand (a stop watch would be ideal)
- Binoculars

Going Ahead

1. Find one or more feeding herons. They like to feed in calm shallow water. Estuaries (the mouth of a river where freshwater mixes with saltwater) are good places to start looking. The beach is another good place to look.
2. For each heron you see feeding, record:
   - the date
   - time
   - location (pool, beach, estuary, etc.).
3. Every time the heron stands still, record:
   - the time before it gives up and walks to a new spot
   - the time it takes to catch a fish
4. Record the total time the heron stays in one area before flying off.
5. Record the total number of fish caught at that place.

6. If you have binoculars (or good eyes), record the number of times the heron strikes but fails to catch a fish.
7. Repeat the observations for as many days and places as possible.
8. Try to deduce any correlation between the time it takes a heron to catch a fish and the time it takes for it to give up and move on. A good way to do this is to draw a graph of one against the other, using all your cases.
9. Can you conclude that the heron 'sizes up' a place based on the time it takes to catch a fish, and moves on when that time is exceeded?

Taking It Further

1. Apply the same observational methods to other animals, say diving ducks. Calculate the average length of time they stay under water during a dive.
   - Is it constant for a particular duck?
   - Is it constant for a particular type of duck?
   - Do other ducks have different averages?
   - Does this average depend on the time of year? How about the distance from the shore? Wave conditions, etc?
   - If possible, score each dive based on whether or not a fish is caught.

Resource Connections

- The Great Blue Heron: A Natural History and Ecology of a Seashore Sentinel by Robert William Butler
- The Patient Predator by Robert William Butler

This activity is based on an idea in the book Beyond Birding: Field Projects for Inquisitive Birders by T. C. Grubb Jr.

33 Messing with Moulds

What's It All About?

Moulds are fungi. But since they don't have a conspicuous fruiting body—like mushrooms—moulds are different from other fungi (see Activity 12 - Mushroom Spore Prints). They grow as branching threads, permeating the substance they grow on and absorbing nutrients from it; to disperse themselves, moulds produce single cells called spores.

Many moulds are parasites, growing on living animals and plants. Many also grow on dead organic material. They hasten the decay process, recycling the nutrients in the ecosystem. Many moulds make chemical compounds that are medically useful, like the antibiotic penicillin and the anti-organ graft rejection drug cyclosporin.

In this activity, you will examine the harmless moulds that live in your community. They are relatively easy to grow and study, and require no specialized equipment. This study will be a simple introduction to microbiological culturing and to microbial biodiversity.

What You Will Need

- A ripe, firm-fleshed melon (like cantaloupe or honeydew)
- Toothpicks
- Q-tips
- Clear flat plastic tubs. Poke a few small holes (about 1 mm diameter) in the lids with a sharp object
- Rubbing alcohol or dilute bleach (1 part water plus 1 part bleach)

Going Ahead

1. It's a good idea to rub the surface of the melon, and the cutting board, with rubbing alcohol or dilute bleach. This procedure kills any fungal spores or bacterial cells that might be lurking on the melon's surface or the cutting surface. It's also a good idea to dip the blade of your knife in alcohol or the dilute bleach for the same reason—allow it to dry before proceeding.

If you decide not to do the sterilization procedures, always include a control slice—one that has not been deliberately inoculated with a prospective fungal sample.

2. Cut some melon slices about 1 cm thick. Store

the rest of the melon in the fridge for later use. Place each slice into a separate tub.

3. Dip the Q-tip in sterile water—water that has been boiled and left to cool in a covered dish. Then sample various areas using wet Q-tips. Remember, mould spores are everywhere. Swipe the Q-tip over the surface of a dusty shelf. Try the shower curtain, the bath tub or the corners of the paint around windows. Outside, try the paint on the north side of the house. Try the surface of a garden path, or the dirt in the garden or the compost heap. Be inventive!

4. Rub your Q-tip over the surface of each melon slice, distributing the sample as well as possible.

5. Put the lids on and store the tubs in a reasonably warm place, out of the direct rays of the sun. The spores will germinate and produce a network of threads in the melon (see 33-1 How Moulds Grow). The mould will use the sugar and other nutrients in the melon as building blocks for its own growth.

6. Observe the slices every day and record what you see. After a few days, a round colony will be visible everywhere that you deposited an unseen spore. Some moulds will grow faster than others.

7. Keep a close eye on the colonies every day. Don't let them get too big because they will produce billions of spores and air currents will waft them into the air, forming colonies on any other slices of melon you are trying to experiment with. Spores are usually visible as a kind of dust that grows on, or just above, the surface of the colony.

8. Record the colour and size of the colonies you see from different samples. Make sketches in your notebook and colour them. Calculate the speed of growth of the different colonies (rate of increase in radius in millimeters per day). Which one is the

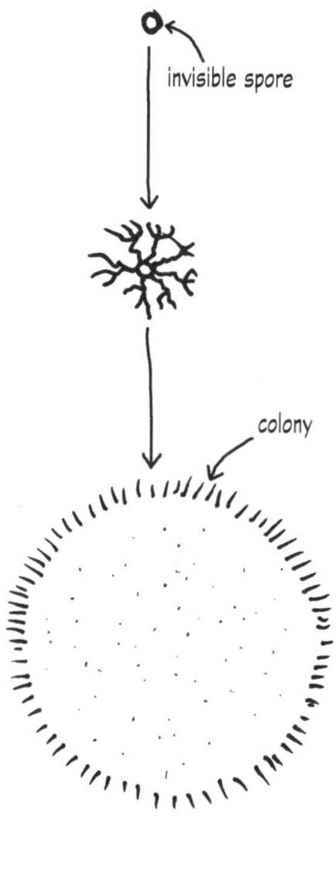

33-1 How Moulds Grow

fastest grower?

9. Do certain types of moulds occur in several samples?

10. Using toothpicks, take a small sample of the main types of colonies and reinoculate them onto fresh slices of melon to obtain 'pure' cultures without other mould types. Do the pure cultures grow faster in the absence of other types?

11. After you have made your observations, dispose of the slices with colonies on them by throwing the whole tub and its contents into the garbage. You can also put the used slice in the composter.

If any members of your family suffer from asthma or allergies to household dust, be especially careful when disposing of the mould-containing slices. Don't allow the spores to get into the air.

Taking It Further

1. Try to inoculate various moulds from the melon slices onto other types of fruit and vegetables. You could inoculate a range of other fruits and vegetables from one distinct colony. Do any of these types of slices provide better growth conditions than the melon? Which types of fruits or vegetables tend to be best?

2. Try to inoculate different moulds in close proximity. Do they grow into each other or maintain a clear zone between them?

3. Try to inoculate colonies onto bread. The bread must be moist; if it is dry, just moisten it with some sterilized water. Compare homemade bread with store-bought bread (which often contains mould retardants). Also try to inoculate onto cold, cooked rice.

4. Try to use spices—curry, mace or cinnamon—as sources of inoculum. Some spices are irradiated

Resource Connections

- What We Find When We Look at Moulds by William Dudley Gray
- Moulds: Their Isolation, Cultivation and Identification by David Malloch

before importation to kill off animals and microbes. However, some may contain spores of foreign moulds from the fields where the spice plants were grown.

5. Try to inoculate moulds into cold, strong tea stored in jars. Tea contains a high concentration of tannin, and one of the few types of moulds capable of growing on it is *Aspergillus niger*—a mould used as a source of several industrial chemicals. *Aspergillus niger* is a black powdery mould.

Discovering Manure Fungi

What's It All About?

Fungi are the decomposers of nature. They break down dead plants and animals, as well as various kinds of solid and liquid animal wastes. They return nutrients to the ecosystem. In this activity, you will focus on fungi that grow on manure.

Different fungi grow at different speeds and some prepare the way for others. When one organism, merely by living in one place, prepares the conditions that make it possible for another organism to live there later, the process is called ecological succession. Succession is a well established general ecological phenomenon that can be observed in many settings.

In this activity, the organisms are fungi living on horse manure. Fungal spores on the grass eaten by a horse survive the journey through its body, and then germinate and grow on the manure.

What You Will Need

- A notebook and pencil
- Extra-large clear plastic bottle
- A manure collection bag (supermarket bags are fine for this)
- Manure from a horse feeding in a field or on hay
- Sticky tape

Going Ahead

1. Cut the top off your bottle and poke a few 1 mm holes in the upper part of the bottle (see 34-1 Growing Manure Fungi).
2. Collect some fresh manure—enough to fill the bottom third of your clear bottle.
3. Tape the bottle top back on—it doesn't have to be a perfect seal
4. Place the bottle in the shade to allow the fungi time to grow. In the summer, place it outside but keep it inside in the winter. The bottle must get some light during the daylight hours. Do not put it in direct sunlight.
5. Watch what happens to the manure. Fungi will start appearing after a few days. Record and describe any and all fungal growth. Record the

date when the growth of one fungal type begins and ends. Draw the fungi that grow.

6. Summarize the entire succession of fungi from beginning to end.

Taking It Further

1. Did the fungal succession in your first experiment occur by chance or was it a biologically inevitable sequence? Explore these questions by repeating the experiment with another sample of manure from the same horse. Then try a different horse from the same field. How about a horse from a different field?
2. Try dung from rabbits, sheep or deer and compare the fungi that grow.
3. Compare the results in all your trials. If you find the same sequence in all cases, record it.
4. You can experiment further by changing the conditions in your bottle.
    - add water so the manure is partially—but not fully—submerged.
    - add a tablespoonful of vinegar mixed with water or a spoonful of baking soda in water.
    - place the manure in the dark.
    - try higher and lower temperatures.

    What happens?
5. Take out some books on fungi from your local library. Can you find the scientific names of fungi that are similar to the ones you observed? If you are unsure, you can just say that a sample "looks like species X."

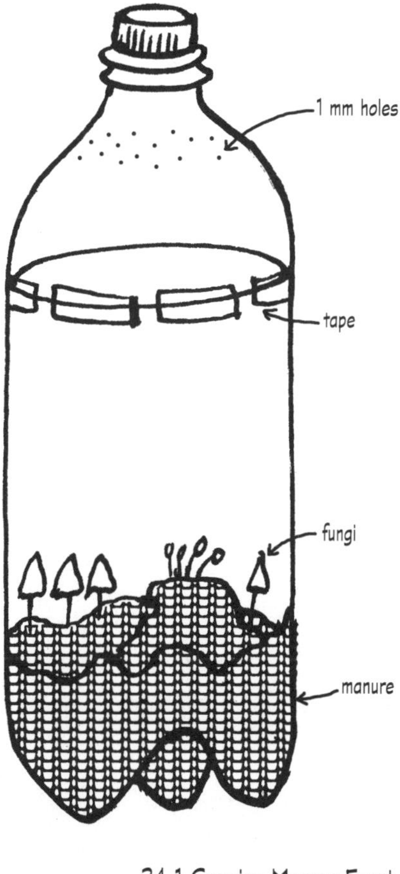

34-1 Growing Manure Fungi

35 Tree Girths

a population study

What's It All About?

In this activity, you will document the sizes of trees in a particular area. Through an analysis of tree size, you'll investigate the ecology and structure of tree populations. You will also get a brief introduction to statistics.

Going Ahead

1. Select a natural wooded area where there are a fair number of trees.
2. Estimate the number of types of trees in the area.
3. Focus on one particular type or species. Examine the trees with the thickest trunks and measure the distance around their trunks—the circumference. As a point of comparison, choose a standard height above the ground—chest height is convenient—and stick to it. Move on to the smaller trees of the same type. Record the measurements of lots of trees, big and small. If possible, try to measure one hundred trees. Don't be selective—your sample should be random.
4. Once you have found the approximate range of tree sizes for a particular species, it might be fun to have a contest to see who can find the thickest tree. Get your friends or family members involved.
5. Chart the results using a bar graph, also called a histogram (see 35-1 Tree Girths). The horizontal axis represents the circumference and the vertical axis represents the number of trees. Choose intervals appropriate for your data (0-50 cm; 51-100 cm; 101-150 cm) so that it's easier to plot the circumference. The length of the bars on the vertical axis should reflect the number of trees in each category.

What You Will Need

- A notebook and pencil
- A long, flexible tape measure (preferably more than 10 metres long)
- Graph or plain paper
- Possibly a tree identification book
- Possibly a saw

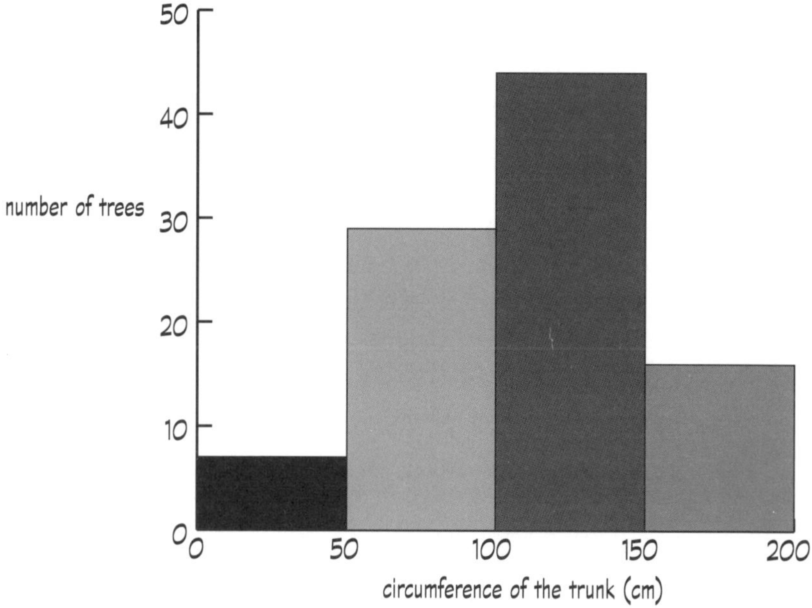

35-1 Tree Girths

6. Questions:
   - What is the average, or mean tree circumference? The average is calculated by adding up all the circumferences and dividing by the total number of trees measured.
   - What is the most common circumference? Is it the same as the average? If not, why not?
   - What are the smallest and the largest recorded circumferences?
   - Make an assessment of the current growth stage of your tree population. Is there a more or less continuous range of sizes (from very large to very small)? If a population is actively regenerating itself, it should contain small seedlings and all tree sizes from there on up. If the range of tree sizes does not extend down to seedling size, the population might not be actively regenerating. Look for clearings caused by windfalls; look at the

edge of the population—are there seedlings in these locations? If so, this might show that regeneration is occurring. No seedlings or the presence of seedlings of another species of tree, might indicate imminent replacement of your tree population by another species. This is called ecological succession. When the present trees reach a certain size, they will die from disease or windfall, and might be replaced by another species. Alder often precedes coniferous species in this way.

Taking It Further

1. Repeat your observations with another tree species in the same wood. Try the second most common. Compare numbers and histograms—are there any differences? If so, suggest a reason.
2. Find a fallen tree, preferably one with a cut end. If you can't find one, cut off the end of a fallen tree with a saw. The aim is to see the growth rings, which are laid down one per year. Counting the number of rings will tell you the age of the tree.
3. Use the information provided by a fallen tree to discover the approximate age of the other trees measured. Begin by measuring the radius of the tree, that is, the distance from the centre of the tree to the outer edge. Use this information to calculate the number of rings per centimetre of radius. (Hint: If there are two rings per centimetre, then this tells you that it took two years for the tree to add one centimetre to its radius.)
4. The original data you collected measured the circumference of the trees, not the radius. It is possible to calculate the radius of the tree

trunks—the relationship between the radius and the circumference is always the same:

- circumference = 2 x π x radius (π is a mathematical constant, approximately 3.14).

Rearranging this formula,

- radius = circumference / 2 x 3.14
  so, radius = circumference / 6.28

If a tree that has a circumference of 73 cm, then it must have a radius of 11.64 cm (73 / 6.28 = 11.64). Since we know that the trees in this area added 1 cm to their circumference every two years, a tree with a radius of 11.64 cm would be approximately 23 years old (11.64 x 2).

You can easily make an age distribution for the trees in your sample by converting all their circumferences to ages!

Curriculum Connections

grade	learning outcomes	activity number											
		1	2	3	4	5	6	7	8	9	10	11	12
K to 1	Following instructions & procedures							✔	✔	✔	✔		✔
	Collaborative scientific investigation	✔	✔	✔	✔	✔	✔	✔	✔	✔	✔	✔	✔
	Interpreting & posing questions				✔	✔	✔	✔	✔		✔	✔	✔
	Describing similarities & differences			✔		✔	✔	✔	✔	✔	✔	✔	✔
	Plant characteristics & diversity of plants in community				✔	✔		✔	✔	✔	✔		✔
	Plant & animal care		✔		✔			✔					
	Animal appearance, behaviour & health	✔	✔	✔									
	Similarities & differences among animal species	✔	✔	✔									
	Plant & animal life cycles		✔					✔	✔				
	Motion & changes in motion												
	Types of forces												
	Variations in patterns												
	Describing & classifying rocks, soil & water						✔						
	Effects of water & wind on rocks & soil						✔						
	The sun & shadows												
2 to 3	Testing & observing										✔		
	Using magnifiers & microscopes		✔					✔					
	Observing, investigating & communicating observations			✔	✔	✔			✔	✔	✔	✔	✔
	Identifying patterns & groupings			✔		✔	✔		✔	✔			✔
	Posing questions for investigation				✔	✔		✔			✔	✔	✔
	Plant survival & plant structures				✔	✔		✔	✔	✔			✔
	Animal survival & animal interactions	✔	✔	✔									
	Comparing & contrasting life cycles of different plants & animals		✔		✔	✔		✔					
	Endangerment & extinction of plant & animal species		✔		✔								
		1	2	3	4	5	6	7	8	9	10	11	12

activity number

13	14	15	16	17	18	19	20	21	22	23	24	25	26	27	28	29	30	31	32	33	34	35
✔	✔	✔	✔			✔	✔		✔	✔				✔							✔	
✔	✔	✔	✔	✔	✔	✔	✔	✔	✔	✔	✔	✔	✔	✔	✔	✔	✔	✔	✔	✔	✔	✔
✔	✔	✔	✔	✔		✔	✔	✔	✔	✔	✔	✔		✔	✔	✔		✔	✔	✔	✔	✔
	✔	✔	✔	✔		✔			✔	✔		✔	✔		✔	✔		✔	✔	✔	✔	✔
				✔				✔		✔					✔	✔						✔
	✔			✔		✔		✔														
	✔					✔					✔							✔	✔			
	✔					✔					✔							✔	✔			
				✔	✔	✔																✔
													✔									
									✔				✔									
												✔										
												✔										
							✔							✔								
	✔	✔				✔	✔		✔	✔	✔									✔	✔	
																				✔		
✔	✔	✔	✔	✔	✔	✔	✔	✔	✔	✔	✔	✔	✔	✔	✔	✔		✔	✔	✔	✔	✔
	✔		✔	✔	✔	✔				✔		✔	✔					✔		✔		✔
✔	✔	✔	✔	✔	✔		✔	✔	✔	✔	✔	✔	✔	✔	✔	✔		✔	✔	✔	✔	✔
				✔	✔			✔							✔							✔
	✔					✔					✔					✔		✔	✔			
				✔	✔													✔				✔
				✔											✔	✔						
13	14	15	16	17	18	19	20	21	22	23	24	25	26	27	28	29	30	31	32	33	34	35

Curriculum Connections

grade	learning outcomes	activity number											
		1	2	3	4	5	6	7	8	9	10	11	12
2 to 3	Hearing & speech												
	Sources and uses of energy												
	Features of the day and night sky												
	Movements of the Earth & day, night & seasons												
	Composition of the Earth						✔						
	Classification & composition of rocks						✔						
4	Predicting & interpreting results							✔			✔	✔	✔
	Performing an experiment							✔			✔		
	Constructing definitions						✔						
	Local organisms in local environments	✔	✔	✔	✔	✔			✔	✔	✔		✔
	Habitat & survival of organisms	✔	✔		✔	✔							
	Life processes of organisms		✔		✔	✔							
	Uses & importance of water		✔										
	Human impact on Earth's water resources												
	Characteristics & uses of simple machines												
5	Designing an experiment							✔			✔		
	Classifying & ordering	✔	✔				✔		✔	✔			
	Technology & humans												
	Use of science in communities												
	Living resources in the local environment & their impacts					✔							
	Human & animal sensory systems	✔									✔		
	Colour & wavelengths												
	Light & vision												
	How non-living resources are used in society												
	Environmental impacts of using non-living resources												
	Natural & synthetic materials												
		1	2	3	4	5	6	7	8	9	10	11	12

activity number

13	14	15	16	17	18	19	20	21	22	23	24	25	26	27	28	29	30	31	32	33	34	35
																		✔				
		✔																				
✔							✔							✔								
✔							✔							✔								
												✔										
												✔										
✔	✔	✔			✔	✔	✔			✔	✔		✔	✔				✔	✔	✔	✔	
	✔	✔				✔				✔	✔		✔					✔		✔	✔	
✔	✔	✔	✔				✔					✔	✔	✔				✔	✔			
	✔			✔		✔		✔			✔				✔	✔	✔	✔				
	✔			✔		✔		✔			✔				✔	✔	✔	✔	✔			
				✔													✔					
		✔																				
		✔																				
													✔									
	✔	✔								✔			✔					✔		✔	✔	
				✔								✔	✔									
		✔			✔				✔				✔									
✔		✔							✔				✔									
									✔													✔
																		✔				
										✔												
										✔												
		✔																				
		✔																				
									✔	✔												
13	14	15	16	17	18	19	20	21	22	23	24	25	26	27	28	29	30	31	32	33	34	35

Curriculum Connections

grade	learning outcomes	activity number											
		1	2	3	4	5	6	7	8	9	10	11	12
6	Using microscopes & instruments of measurement		✔					✔					
	Drawing conclusions & explaining hypotheses							✔			✔		
	Organizing & interpreting information												
	Comparing ways of problem-solving												
	Plant & animal classification	✔	✔			✔		✔	✔	✔			✔
	Plant & animal cells							✔	✔				
	Effects of micro-organisms on other organisms		✔										
	Human defenses against harmful micro-organisms												
	Types of forces												
	Relationship among forces, motion, mass												
	Relationship of movement of sun, moon & Earth												
7	Experimenting & investigating	✔	✔	✔	✔	✔	✔	✔	✔	✔	✔	✔	✔
	Evaluating conclusions & summarizing data							✔	✔		✔		
	Relating technology & science												
	Relating science to community	✔	✔	✔	✔	✔	✔	✔	✔	✔	✔	✔	✔
	Food webs & species interactions	✔	✔										
	Comparing & contrasting biogeoclimatic zones of BC					✔							✔
	Plant & animal reproduction	✔	✔	✔	✔	✔		✔					
	Growth & development of organisms	✔	✔		✔	✔		✔					
	Factors influencing length & quality of life of organisms							✔					
		1	2	3	4	5	6	7	8	9	10	11	12

activity number

13	14	15	16	17	18	19	20	21	22	23	24	25	26	27	28	29	30	31	32	33	34	35
✔							✔													✔		
	✔	✔	✔		✔	✔	✔	✔		✔	✔		✔	✔				✔	✔	✔	✔	
			✔				✔	✔				✔						✔				
		✔	✔		✔								✔									
				✔													✔					✔
																				✔	✔	
																				✔	✔	
					✔				✔				✔									
					✔		✔		✔				✔									
✔							✔							✔								
✔	✔	✔	✔	✔	✔	✔	✔	✔	✔	✔	✔	✔	✔	✔	✔	✔	✔	✔	✔	✔	✔	✔
	✔	✔	✔		✔	✔	✔	✔		✔	✔			✔				✔	✔	✔	✔	
		✔			✔				✔				✔									
✔	✔	✔	✔	✔	✔	✔	✔	✔	✔	✔	✔	✔	✔	✔	✔	✔	✔	✔	✔	✔	✔	✔
											✔						✔		✔			
				✔													✔					✔
																						✔
				✔																		✔
13	14	15	16	17	18	19	20	21	22	23	24	25	26	27	28	29	30	31	32	33	34	35

Curriculum Connections

grade	learning outcomes	activity number											
		1	2	3	4	5	6	7	8	9	10	11	12
7	Evolution of human understanding of the universe through time												
	How earthquakes & volcanoes change the Earth's surface						✔						
	Geological features of the ocean floor & surface of continents						✔						

activity number																						
13	14	15	16	17	18	19	20	21	22	23	24	25	26	27	28	29	30	31	32	33	34	35
							✔															

BC Hydro

http://www.bchydro.com/education has activities on electricity, energy conservation, determining your energy footprint, the environment, renewable and non-renewable energy.

Burns Bog Conservation Society

202-11961 88th Avenue
Delta, BC V4C 3C9
Tel: (604) 572-0373
Fax: (604) 572-0374
Email: burnsbog@uniserve.com
URL: http://www.burnsbog.paconline.net

- Summer day camps in Burns Bog and tours of the conservation area.

Capilano Salmon Hatchery

4500 Capilano Park Road
Tel: (604) 666-1790
Fax: (604) 666-1949
URL: http://habitat.pac.dfo.ca/heb/faculties/capilano/default/htm
North Vancouver, BC V7R 4L3

- Open year-round. Self-guided tours available.

Central Okanagan Science Opportunities for Kids Society

Tel: (250) 736-4427
Fax: (250) 860 6622 or 763-4427 (call first)
Email: jfrench@silk.net
URL: http://www.geocities.com/CapeCanaveral/Hall/3444

- Provides hands-on science experiences for elementary school-aged children in the Okanagan through classroom presentations, community science programs after school and on weekends and summer and spring break science camps.

City Farmer/Vancouver Compost Demonstration Garden

2150 Maple Street
Vancouver, BC V6J 1T3
Tel: (604) 736-2250
Fax: (604) 685-5832
Email: cityfarm@interchange.ubc.ca
URL: www.cityfarmer.org

- Offers workshops and tours where families can learn about organic gardening, as well as composting.

Courtenay & District Museum & Paleontology Centre

360 Cliffe Avenue
Courtenay, BC V9N 2H9
Tel: (250) 334-3611
Fax: (250) 334-4277
Email: museum@island.net
URL: http://www.courtenaymuseum.bc.ca

- School and public tours of paleontology, geology, basic archaeology. Includes field trips to local river fossil formations and a geological trip to Comox Lake.

EcoWatch

www.cciw.ca/ecowatch/introduction.html

- EcoWatch provides hands-on experience of collecting environmental monitoring data for youth. The data collected by volunteer community members (i.e. students, families, etc.) can be used by scientists to further their investigations about ecosystems. EcoWatch links to on-line environmental programs like Amphibian Watch and Plant Watch. EcoWatch is a component of EMAN (Ecological Monitoring and Assessement Network of Environment Canada).

Eureka Science

University College of the Cariboo, Kamloops, BC

Phone: (250) 371-5534

Email: eureka@cariboo.bc.ca

- Summer science camps for kids. Run by undergraduate engineering and science students.

Forest Alliance of British Columbia

PO Box 49312 1055 Dunsmuir Street

Vancouver, BC V7X 1L3

Tel: 1 (800) 567 TREE

URL: http://www.forest.org

- Liaises with companies offering sawmill tours, pulp and paper mill tours and woods tours at over 40 locations around BC. Pre-booking is required.

Fraser-Fort George Regional Museum

333 Gorse Street in Fort George Park

Prince George, BC

Tel: (250) 562-1612

Fax: (250) 562-6395

Email: info@museum.princegeorge.com

URL. www.museum@princegeorge.com

- Offers various science education programs in a hands-on science gallery, open to the public.
- Summer camps available in July and August through Science Alliance (Email: camps@museum.princegeorge.com).

GEERing UP!

University of British Columbia, Vancouver, BC
Tel: (604) 822-2858
Email: GEERingUp@apsc.ubc.ca

- Summer science camps for kids

Go West

University of Victoria
Tel: (250) 721-8983
Fax: (250) 721-8676
Email: go-west@engr.uvic.ca
URL: http://www.engr.uvic.ca/~go-west

- Summer youth programs (grades 10-12).

Greater Vancouver Zoo

5048 264th Street
Aldergrove, BC V4W 1N7
Tel: (604) 856-6825
Fax: (604) 857-9008

- Open to the public 365 days a year.
- Sleepover program for groups.

GVRD

4330 Kingsway
Burnaby, BC V5H 4G8
Tel: (604) 432-6339
Fax: (604) 436-6811
bweber@gvrd.bc.ca
Compost Hotline: (604) 736-2250
Recycling Hotline: 732-9253 or 1 800 667-4321
URL: http://www.gvrd.bc.ca

- Backyard and work composting workshops from March through November, free to GVRD residents.

Kootenay Gallery of Art, History and Science

120 Heritage Way (across from Castlegar airport)
Castlegar, BC
Tel: (250) 365-3337
Fax: (250) 365-3822
Email: kgal@netidea.com

- Hosts traveling exhibitions featuring first regional, then provincial, national, and international exhibits. Admission by donation.

Let's Talk Science

c/o Office of the Registrar, SFU
Burnaby, BC V6T 1Z1
Tel: (604) 268-6583
Fax: (604) 268-6584
URL: http://www.letstalkscience.uwo.ca

- Offers workshops and demonstrations for classrooms, home schoolers, summer camps. Adventures in Science program provides evening hands-on activities for members of Girl Guides and Scouts Canada. The Canadian Association for Girls in Science is a club for girls who like science and want to learn more. Ages 7-16.

Lower Seymour Conservation Reserve

(formerly Seymour Demonstration Forest)
Tel: (604) 987-1273
The LSCR is a 5600 hectare open watershed, managed by the GVRD for the future storage of drinkwater

- Summer camps for kids, weekend education programs for families, free Sunday tours.

Lynn Canyon Ecology Centre

Located at the foot of Peters Rd, Lynn Valley
North Vancouver, BC.
Tel: (604) 981-3103
Fax: (604) 981-3154
Email: ecocnter@wimsey.com
URL: http://www.dnv.org/parks/funparks.htm

- Ecology Centre open to public by donation.

Mad Science

Tel: 1 (877) 900-9996
URL: http://www.madscience.com

- Franchises in the Lower Mainland, Vancouver Island, and Fraser Valley; offers science demonstrations and activities to birthday parties, Brownies, Cubs and other local groups.

National Research Council of Canada

5071 West Saanich Road
Victoria, BC V8X 4M6
Tel: (250) 363-0001
Fax: (250) 363-0045
Email: jaques.vallee@hia.nrc.ca

- Free self-guided tours weekdays of the biggest telescope and dome in BC (and 2nd biggest in Canada). Also self-guided tours of surrounding exhibits. During summer, free Saturday evening telescope shows.

NORTHWEST WILDLIFE PRESERVATION SOCIETY

707-1112 West Pender St
Vancouver, BC V6E 2S1
Tel: (604) 713-6686
Fax: (604) 713-6698
Email: nwps@direct.ca
URL: http://mypage.direct.ca/nwps

- Wildlife and habitat presentations, $75 each, for all ages.
- Grasslands youth stewardship program.
- Estuaries stewardship program, for all ages.

OWL (ORPHANED WILDLIFE) REHABILITATION SOCIETY

3800 72nd Street
Delta, BC V4K 3N2
Tel: (604) 946-3171
Fax: (604) 946-3172
Email: OWL_REHAB@bc.sympatico.ca
URL: www.realm.ca/owl

- Tours Saturday and Sunday 10-3. Call in advance.

PACIFIC SPACE CENTRE AND CANADIAN SPACE RESOURCE CENTRE

1100 Chestnut Street
Vancouver, BC V6J 3J9
Tel: (604) 738-7827
Fax: (604) 736-5665
URL: http://pacific-space-centre.bc.ca

Parents for Science Society

Parents for Science Society is a volunteer-based association of parents sharing a concern for the science education of children. Contact Minty Thompson at (604) 737-0887, or at minty@dowco.com.

Reifel Migratory Bird Sanctuary

5191 Robertson Road
Delta, BC V4K 3N2
Tel: (604) 946-6980
Fax: (604) 946-6980

- Guided tours for pre-booked groups. Open to the public.

Richmond Nature Park Society

11851 Westminster Hwy
Richmond, BC V6X 1B4
Tel: (604) 273-7015
Fax: (604) 279-9358
Email: kbauder@city.richmond.bc.ca

- Nature interpretation, individuals, groups, $3/person year-round.
- Nature interpretation, drop-in, free, Sundays.
- Interpretation/Visitor centre, free, daily, year-round.

Royal Astronomical Society of Canada (Vancouver Centre)

109-2330 Maple Street
Vancouver, BC V6J 3T6
Tel: (604) 734-9726
Fax: (604) 734-9726
Email: dmunro@sfu.ca

Science AL!VE

888 University Drive
Simon Fraser University
Burnaby, BC V5A 1S6
Te;: (604) 291-5912
Email: yescamps@sfu.ca
URL: http://www.sfu.ca.science-alive

- Summer science camps for kids.

Science Venture

University of Victoria, Victoria, BC
Tel: (250) 721-8661
Fax: (250) 721-8676
Email: sventure@engr.uvic.ca
URL: http://www.engr.uvic.ca/~sventure

- Summer day camps for kids entering grades 3-9. Run by undergraduate engineering and science students.

Science World

1455 Quebec Street
Vancouver, BC V6A 3Z7
Tel: (604) 268-6363
Fax: (604) 682-2923
URL: www.scienceworld.bc.ca

Stanley Park Ecology Society

Dining Pavilion
PO Box 5167 Vancouver, BC V6B 4B2
Tel: (604) 257-6907
Fax: (604) 257-8378
URL: http://www.oroad.com/spes

- Classroom programs with fee.

Swan Lake Christmas Hill Nature Sanctuary

3873 Swan Lake Rd.
Victoria, BC V8X 3W1
Tel: (250) 479-0211
Fax: (250) 479-0132
Email: tmorrison@swanlake.bc.ca
URL: http://www.swanlake.bc.ca

- Public programs during school breaks, weekends. Birdwalks twice weekly. Summer nature camps. Walking trails.

University of British Columbia Botanical Garden

6804 S.W. Marine Drive
Vancouver, BC
Tel: (604) 822-9666

- Plant biodiversity, walking trails, gift shop, annual native plant sales.

University of British Columbia Physics Outreach Lab

6224 Agricultural Road
Vancouver, BC V6T 1Z1
Tel: (604) 822-3675
Fax: (604) 822-5324
Email: outreach@physics.ubc.ca
URL: www.physics.ubc.ca/~outreach/home.htm

- Physics summer camps for kids aged 6-16.

Vancouver Aquarium Marine Science Centre

845 Avison Way
PO Box 3232
Vancouver, BC V6B 3X8
Tel: (604) 659-3474
Fax: (604) 631-2529
Email: education@vanaqua.org
URL: www.vanaqua.org

- Call the info line at (604) 659-3474 or visit the website for up-to-date listings of available programs.

Vancouver Museum

1100 Chestnut Street
Vancouver, BC V6J 3J6
Tel: (604) 736-4431
Fax: (604) 736-5417
Email: edoyle@vanmuseum.bc.ca
URL: http://www.vanmuseum.bc.ca

- Opening a large exhibition about biodiversity in March 2000. Kids camps associated with it.

VanDusen Botanical Garden

5251 Oak Street
Vancouver, BC
Tel: (604) 878-9274
URL: http://www.vandusengarden.org

- Family adventures every month including seasonal nature walks, bird walks, Pond Peering and Trees Please.
- Engaging curriculum-linked school programs during school season.
- For more information check out our web site.

Victoria Lapidary and Mineral Society

Tel: (250) 658-5503

Fax: (250) 475-6896

Email: johnirene@home.com

URL: http://www.islandnet.com/~vlms

- Offers earth science workshops.

About APASE

Science surrounds us. Understanding science helps us understand ourselves and our world. Our goal is to provide equitable resources that invite curiosity and enrich the life of our communities through science education. We are the Association for the Promotion and Advancement of Science Education (APASE) and we are dedicated to building sustainable communities through science education. We emphasize the ways in which science and technology contribute to the quality of our lives and impact our everyday experiences.

Our programs inspire innovation and lifelong learning in the realm of science education. We offer a diverse range of services. Our science workshops and publications for families, elementary school teachers and students emphasize hands-on, discovery-based learning and mentorship. We are actively involved in BC's adult English-as-a-second-language (ESL) community, promoting environmental citizenship. Our new media projects include an online curriculum, a linked environmental education resource for K-7 teachers and an exciting science mystery game for children.

Founded in 1983, APASE is a registered charity and non-profit society, dedicated to supporting teachers, parents and other community role models in capturing the interests of elementary school children. As a past winner of the Michael Smith Award for Excellence in Science Promotion and the VanCity Environmental Educator's Award, our work is provincially and nationally recognized.

About the authors

Dr. Anthony Griffiths, the primary author, is a geneticist in the Department of Botany at the University of British Columbia. The other authors and contributors are scientists, engineers and science educators.

- APASE: Association for the Promotion and
  Advancement of Science Education
  Telephone: (604) 687-8712
  Fax: (604) 687-8715
  Email: info@apase.bc.ca
  www.apase.bc.ca